AFTER TROY

Glyn Maxwell

AFTER TROY

OBERON BOOKS
LONDON

First published in 2011 by Oberon Books Ltd
521 Caledonian Road, London N7 9RH
Tel: +44 (0) 20 7607 3637 / Fax: +44 (0) 20 7607 3629
e-mail: info@oberonbooks.com
www.oberonbooks.com

A catalogue record for this book is available from the British
Library.

ISBN: 978-1-84943-026-5

Cover design by Reg Schleiger

Printed in Great Britain
by Marston Book Services Limited, Didcot.

The author would like to thank the following for their significant contribution to the development of this play at workshop and draft stage: Jack Bradley, Tom Burke, Jennifer Kidd, Laura Martin Simpson, Madlena Nedeva, Pippa Nixon, Richard Riddell, James Russell, Lucy Voller and Robin Whiting.

Characters

HECUBA
Queen of Troy, widow of Priam

ANDROMACHE
widow of Hecuba's son Hector

POLYXENA
daughter of Hecuba

CASSANDRA
daughter of Hecuba

AGAMEMNON
King of Mycenae, Greece

TALTHYBIUS
his scribe

MESTOR
King of the isle of Mestor

KRATOS
a soldier

Troy has fallen to the Greeks. Its men are dead,
its women are in prison.

Note
The dialogue in bold type is Cassandra in exact unison
with whoever is speaking.

After Troy was first performed in March 2011 at the Playhouse Theatre Oxford, with the following cast (in order of appearance):

KRATOS, Iain Batchelor
TALTHYBIUS, Oscar Pearce
HECUBA, Eve Matheson
POLYXENA, Amy Noble
ANDROMACHE, Hannah Barrie
CASSANDRA, Rebecca Smith-Williams
AGAMEMNON, Antony Byrne
MESTOR, Nicolas Tennant

Director, Alex Clifton
Designer, Patrick Burnier
Composer, Alex Silverman
Lighting Designer, Mike Gunning
Movement Director, Kate Flatt
Dramaturg, Jack Bradley

After Troy was produced by Lifeblood Theatre Company in association with The Onassis Programme.

ACT ONE

A cave with two entrances. A 'light' way leads outside, a 'dark' way to further caves. Pre-dawn light on three sleeping women, HECUBA and POLYXENA together, ANDROMACHE to one side. A fourth bed is empty.

KRATOS is standing among the beds, looking at the women. TALTHYBIUS comes, with a lamp. A gust of wind.

KRATOS	A breeze. We're going home.
TALTHYBIUS	Who are you? Are you standing there for a reason?
KRATOS	The wind blew.
TALTHYBIUS	Were you ordered to stand here?
KRATOS	You sound like *they* do.
TALTHYBIUS	What?
KRATOS	Always questions. *Where'd you come from, why'd you come from there,* *why don't you leave, are you leaving,* *when are you leaving?* I go: *I'm Kratos the Greek* that's all they need to know.
TALTHYBIUS	Who sent you? Who's in command of you?
KRATOS	Always questions. You're like these Trojan ladies, secretary. Look, there's an empty bed, you can lie down, think up your next question.
TALTHYBIUS	I'm a scribe not a secretary. I answer to Agamemnon. Whose empty bed is that?
KRATOS	That would be Dead-Eyes.
TALTHYBIUS	Who's 'Dead-Eyes'?
KRATOS	That's Dead-Eyes, right there, you can't see her, she's out there with the army, telling tales for chicken bones.
TALTHYBIUS	Cassandra.

KRATOS	Can't even say the names, they're not like our names.
	Their language, *that* I get,
	Greek as said by drunks, or girls so drunk
	they sing a song about it, but the names…
	This one's called Moonface. *[ANDROMACHE]*
	This one's called Biter. *[POLYXENA]*
TALTHYBIUS	They're not called that.
KRATOS	By me they are, I name them, I'm a Greek,
	I mark the spot.
TALTHYBIUS	This child is a princess,
	Polyxena. This one's Andromache
	the widow of Hector. Try it: An-*drom*-a-kee.
	It would help if you could say it.
KRATOS	I could say it. –
TALTHYBIUS	This is the Queen of Troy.
KRATOS	The queen of where?
	What's she queen of now? She's queen of that lot.

KRATOS gestures out through the dark exit.

TALTHYBIUS	How many lie in there?
KRATOS	I don't *go* in there
	so I'm lying if I tell you. Forty odd?
	But *they* don't speak at all, them dogs and cats.
TALTHYBIUS	There was a breeze. When the wind picks up tomorrow
	we will depart forthwith. These royal captives
	will be housed here in the garrison. In time
	I imagine they'll be free to go.
KRATOS	I imagine
	you do.
TALTHYBIUS	We need to wake them.
KRATOS	Good luck.
TALTHYBIUS	We need to wake them now.
KRATOS	They sleep till sunrise.
	On account of what we call the mercy water.
TALTHYBIUS	What did you say?
KRATOS	I said: the mercy water.

TALTHYBIUS	Mercy water – you mean you drug these women?
KRATOS	A mercy to the ears of the whole camp.
	Sunset lights them up, they *change*,
	they move and sort of sway – I'd call it *dance*
	but I like a dance and I don't like what they do
	so I don't call it dance. They sing a song
	of stuff that isn't there, *she* makes a sound
	she made before, then *this one* makes a sound
	that sounds just like a sound *she* made, it's murder
	I'm telling you, they'll do it at sunrise
	but we can drown that out, small bloody mercy.
TALTHYBIUS	Disgraceful.
KRATOS	You should hear it.
TALTHYBIUS	That you drug them
	is disgraceful. It's unwarranted, ignoble.
KRATOS	It's alright, mister scribe, few more long words,
	sun'll be up in no time. Look it's moving,
	old Mother Rat.
HECUBA *[in sleep]*	*O, open the curtains…*
TALTHYBIUS	What did she say?
KRATOS	She does this every morning.
HECUBA *[in sleep]*	*I'd rather the blue sash*
	than the golden sash the blue sash…
KRATOS	Oh would you?
TALTHYBIUS	Don't touch her.
KRATOS	I'm not touching her. I choose
	not to, she's not clean. Where it's not clean
	the rats come. What you saying, Mother Rat?
TALTHYBIUS	She's in the time before.
KRATOS	It's ten weeks,
	Mother Rat, ten weeks this little shit-hole's
	been the whole of Troy!
HECUBA *[in sleep]*	*O Thou,*
	Thou of Light and Music…
KRATOS	No one's here,
	Mother Rat, just me!

TALTHYBIUS	She's praying, fool.
KRATOS	Who's 'Thou of Light and Music'?
TALTHYBIUS	It's Apollo.
	They never say the names.
KRATOS	You don't say.
	No wonder the gods don't know them.
TALTHYBIUS	Oh indeed,
	and they shower us with blessings.
KRATOS	They do.
	They keep on our right side. Only joking.
TALTHYBIUS	She's waking up. Leave them. I said leave them.

TALTHYBIUS and KRATOS leave the women alone. Faint morning light.

HECUBA wakes, and pieces together fragments. What she heard in half-sleep is translated into signs. The dream is still in the cave with her.

HECUBA   Music, Light and Poetry you left here
very lately, did you… I know you…
you left your light with me, you told me more…
My sleeping angel smiles in sleep, she knows *[POLYXENA]*
you breathed here by our bedsides…
Andromache's cheeks are always dry by morning.

Thou of Light and Medicine you left me
dreams…Greeks were there, the morning light
blushes to admit it, Greeks were there,
one clouded up the sky, he had no name
history will remember, am I right,
Thou of Oracles? The light agrees,
agrees, and grows. They will not be remembered.

A lantern flickered here – here –
you sent it, Thou of Knowledge.
I was in my chamber then,
in the afternoon we span in our new robes
for we would dance that night! *Evan Evoe!*
That they were gone! That they

12

were gone away and Troy
was shimmering in the evening light! No dream,
Thou of Light, no dream but what's to come!

For dreams are signs, I know this…
I was, they said, an educated princess
but shy…Dreams are only how you tell me,
how you tell me what will come,
Thou of Light and Music,
what will be done for us,
what will be done to them
who came. Such misery will rain upon them
I almost find some pity for them! At least
I look, if I don't find.

She paces the cave, points to where KRATOS *was, and where* TALTHYBIUS
was.

HECUBA   The dark figure feared me in the dream,
          but the light figure (Thou of Light, I know you)
          he knew me for the Queen of Troy, I asked him
          for the blue sash, the blue is the horizon,
          not the golden sash, the golden sash is fire
          at the marble gate and – bodies standing staring –
          three tiny voices begging under tables…
          my darling, Priam, kneeling and explaining
          I am outnumbered, love…I am – outnumbered…
          The blue sash, horizon, the ocean…
          they will stand on the horizon, you have told me,
          Thou of Light and Oracle and Knowing,
          those who swore they would deliver us,
          the lords of the far islands,
          and at the plunging prow and the rising prow
          of the silver ship that is the first we glimpse,
          my – Palidorus, ah my Palidorus,
          my child, my prince of Troy! Ah, I saw you!

O, what I have lost is lost,
O my Priam, O my Hector,
my Paris, all my boy-kings,
but the survivors muster in the mountains
watching for the fleet!
What is to come must be
and it is sailing and in dreams you show me
nightly! Troy, Troy,
we must sing you as you are, so, one morning,
my fatherless poor son
forlorn on a grey sea,
he blinks and blinks again,
for there fall *two* drops of light,
a jewel of pink on both his eyes, it's dawn
anointing the far towers of his birthplace!
Then he roars back from the deck
to the fleet of all who love us, and he cries
I see her, it is Troy, it is still standing!

HECUBA rises. She starts to stamp a rhythm on the floor. From the further cave, we hear the sound of the SHADOW-WOMEN, stamping and moaning in lamentation, over which HECUBA begins her Song of Troy.

HECUBA   *I stroll out in the morning sun!*
                           I stroll out in the morning sun!

Groggy and half-dreaming, POLYXENA and ANDROMACHE wake.

POLYXENA   I dream of him I always dream…
HECUBA   *I stroll out in the morning sun!*
ANDROMACHE   I dreamed of him I always dream…
POLYXENA   *I stroll out in the morning sun*
HECUBA   *We gossip by the Diamond Gate*

All the WOMEN dance.

POLYXENA   *We gossip by the Diamond Gate…*
                           I'm always early, always late!
                           Andromache, Andromache,
                           I'm who you see!

ANDROMACHE	*I'm who you see!*
	I'm walking down Winemakers Street
POLYXENA	*Your silver sandals on your feet!*
HECUBA	*And all the world is passing by*
POLYXENA	*And all my friends, and I, and I –*
	I'm late for school, I'm on the Square,
	People are there, people are everywhere!
ANDROMACHE	Too long, Polyxena.
POLYXENA	But it's many people!
HECUBA	*The temple steps are ninety-one*
POLYXENA	*I reach the top, then down I run!*
ANDROMACHE	*I turn round on the highest step*
	And see the golden town
POLYXENA	Too short,
	Andromache!
ANDROMACHE	It took my breath away
	seeing it all at once.
HECUBA	Go on!
	The world is all before you!
ANDROMACHE	*The…altar sides are nine men high*
HECUBA	*And murals of the starry sky*
POLYXENA	*The boys will swim and so shall I!*
ANDROMACHE	What, from the top of the temple?
POLYXENA	I'm not *there* now,
	I'm by the lucky stream,
	they push me in the water!
ANDROMACHE	Fine, why not,
	what's next…
POLYXENA	*The sun is in the sky…*
	The boys will swim and so shall I
	All afternoon don't ask me why!
HECUBA	*The old men drinking in the shade*
ANDROMACHE	*The horse he rode, the place I laid*
HECUBA	*On the far bank the children played*
POLYXENA	*And I come home to – what? Oh no I lose!*
HECUBA	Polyxena, you're hopeless.

15

POLYXENA   I'm not hopeless,
                        am I hopeless, mother?
HECUBA   Of course not.
POLYXENA   Bracelet of gold!

HECUBA raises POLYXENA's arm, with a golden bracelet; their arms entwine.

HECUBA   Bracelet of silver.
HECUBA/POLYXENA   *When Polyxena sings*
                            Then Palidorus smiles

They embrace. CASSANDRA comes, dishevelled, through the light entrance.

POLYXENA   Cassandra's here, where were you, what's happened?
CASSANDRA   True, gone, and everything.
POLYXENA   Lie down,
                        you have to sleep sometimes.
CASSANDRA   I am asleep.
                        He's here, when I'm asleep he's always here
                        so I *am* and he is here.
POLYXENA   Who is, Old Cass?

CASSANDRA covers one of her eyes.

CASSANDRA   *One eye open, one eye not.*
POLYXENA   There's nobody we know like that.
CASSANDRA   He's here,
                        I saw him, I said *Why is your blind eye crying*
                        when it can't see what was done?
POLYXENA   I don't like riddles.
                        I mean I do, I just don't like other people's.
                        We were singing the morning song!
                        Andromache climbed the temple steps,
                        then I was in the stream, they pushed me in!
                        Mother, where were you?
HECUBA   I was here in Troy.
POLYXENA   In the *song* where were you?
HECUBA   I was here in Troy.

POLYXENA *[To CASS]* Tell me the story you tell me. How does it start…
One day, in a far-off country…

POLYXENA and CASSANDRA go aside.

HECUBA He was here again. I saw him. Palidorus.
He stood right there. I saw his silver bracelet
catch the moonlight.

ANDROMACHE Moonlight? This is a cave,
Hecuba.

HECUBA So is the mind a cave
when the light is gone. I won't tell my daughters.
They'd cry in ecstasy and all the Greeks
would know what's coming to them.

ANDROMACHE Nothing's coming.
The world has come already. What do they want,
the moon and stars? Or did they melt them down
for campaign medals? Give them a badge. Ten years
to think of one dirty trick.

HECUBA Palidorus,
I saw him, and he spoke.

ANDROMACHE In a dream he spoke.
I had a dream. I knew it was a dream,
because it had come before, like some doddering poet
who thinks he's never sung this one when he's sung it
every night for weeks. But oh I'll have it,
poet, as I love it. Hector came home
so filthy he was gleaming,
but we couldn't wait and by the time the sun rose
sideways, like a crab goes,
to warn me I was dreaming,
I was filthy too, *I* was gleaming
and we both woke up and Hector wasn't there.

HECUBA My poor child.

ANDROMACHE Oh and *he* wasn't there either.

HECUBA I mean my son.

ANDROMACHE I too mean my son.

You mean your child and I mean my child.
We always mean the same, you and I.
We mean the sun's come up and life is over.

HECUBA   Hector was my son.

ANDROMACHE   He was my life,
and that's what I call a dream,
but that's *all* I call it, Hecuba.

HECUBA   My son,
Palidorus, last Prince of Troy,
is in the keeping of the island king.
He sailed there long ago.

ANDROMACHE   Lucky him. *My* son,
the other 'last Prince of Troy', Astyanax,
is in the hands of Greeks.

HECUBA   Your child is safe.
He of Knowledge told me.

ANDROMACHE   Did he really.
Can She of Mercy let me see his face?

HECUBA   I shall ask her when I see her.

ANDROMACHE   Would you do that?
Good, because the gods who I've been begging
are She of the Folded Arms and He of Grinning.

HECUBA   The gods have never left me. They tell me
all that is to come. In the woods and hills
our warriors who fled that night are gathered,
watching for the signal. He of Light
reveals to me Prince Palidorus, sailing,
for Mestor, the King of the Stone Island,
swore oaths upon the lives of his own sons
that if terror came to Troy then every island
would rise against the Greeks.

ANDROMACHE   Terror came
and Terror went and islands are islands.

HECUBA   A fleet of a thousand ships will sail.

ANDROMACHE   What signal
are they waiting for? Troy's not a city.

	It's a hippodrome of soot and some high fences.
HECUBA	The city stands. Greeks may slouch within it
	but the city stands, it is shown to me in dreams.
ANDROMACHE	Why do you think they keep us in this hole?
HECUBA	They are ashamed, they keep us out of sight.
	We remind them they are brutes.
ANDROMACHE	So we're the bones
	a dog will bury.
HECUBA	Andromache!
ANDROMACHE	Or the shit.
HECUBA	Nobody listen to her.
ANDROMACHE	Why do you think
	the soldiers bind our eyes when they let us up there?
HECUBA	We can't hear you.
ANDROMACHE	Because we'd gouge them out
	if we saw what's left. Because what's left is nothing.
	Ten weeks and still they walk us in a circle,
	and the ladies howl their husbands' names. Do *you*
	hear an echo? If the days had walls
	there'd be an echo, Hecuba. There's just
	air the Greeks infect.
HECUBA	Because
	you will not hear the gods, Andromache,
	it does not mean we are forgotten.
ANDROMACHE	No.
	Our names comes up and the Immortals chuckle.
	Troy was some prank at school. Well I liked my dream,
	I'll go home to it. Hey look, I'm dressed for it.

ANDROMACHE goes back to bed. HECUBA sits alone.

POLYXENA	That was a perfect story. So she was happy,
	the girl in the story, with the man she married?
CASSANDRA	She was never sad again. She was both sad,
	and never again.
POLYXENA	I'm sad it's just a story.
	I wish it was just all true. I wish sometimes

> you said things that were real, like in the world.
> Sleep's what you need, Old Cass,
> and I'll tell you my secret story.

CASSANDRA lies back in POLYXENA's arms, and closes her eyes.

POLYXENA   There was once a girl, not me, but my age,
and she lived in the city of – Tree, which I've made up.
Did I tell this tale before?

CASSANDRA   Yes and no.

POLYXENA   They were having a war with the Army of the – Freaks,
and the Freaks destroyed their homes. Some of the Freaks
were evil, but there was one of them, whose name
was – well, it began with…

*CASSANDRA, eyes shut, draws an '**a**' in the air.*

POLYXENA   Yes! I must have told you…

CASSANDRA   Yes and no.

POLYXENA   *That* sign, it stood for being the mightiest man
in all the army of them. He wasn't evil,
he was beautiful, he might have been quite evil
sometimes but he needed to be sometimes.
In the story. So, one day the Freaks all came
to the Temple of She of Wisdom, and all
the important Freaks and all the important – Treejans
met to talk about War. And the beautiful Freak
beginning with *[she signs '**a**']* did meet the girl in the story,
and She of Beauty smiled on that moment,
and She of Memory smiles on it still,
in the story, this all is. And she had a bracelet
in the story, like this bracelet in real life,
it was gold, it was wrought for her on Crystal Square
when she was young, her brother Palid –
no, *Peligorus* – got a silver one
and they swore to wear their bracelets to the world's end!
The end of *that* world, I mean, which I've made up
and can end at any time…
Did I tell this tale before?

CASSANDRA   Yes and no.

POLYXENA   Well the beautiful Freak warrior took a knife
and carved *[she and CASS sign '**a**']* in the gold
because he was strong enough he could *carve gold*,
and *[she and CASS sign '**a**']* means the beginning of all things
in the language of the Freaks. And she wore it always.
When the war was over, she was a royal captive,
and he was most likely injured from his wounds,
but he came at last to lead her far away
like in your story, Cass, so my story ends
quite like yours, because she was always happy
and was never sad again, like you say:
she was sad, but never again. But it's just a story
quite like yours.

ANDROMACHE   More Greeks on the horizon.

TALTHYBIUS and KRATOS come through the light entrance. KRATOS goes on through the dark exit.

TALTHYBIUS   *Hek*-yu-bah. An-*drom*-a-kee.
Po-*lyx*-i-na. Your names there. This one.   *[CASSANDRA]*
Best not to disturb… I hope you are well
this morning, ladies, if I *might*
intrude on your, your time. It is good news!
The wind blew! A little breeze, last night.
Thought I'd forgotten the sound of wind! When I heard it
I wanted to write it down, but – how would you spell it?
With a *wh* perhaps, and a – well.
One can't say everything. But what this means is,
preparations are now underway
for our homeward departure. And what *that* means is,
you will soon be rehoused, re – resettled,
in your new quarters…

ANDROMACHE   I want to see my son,
Astyanax, I was assured he's safe,
I want to see him now!

TALTHYBIUS   As indeed you will!

I am instructed to escort, forthwith,
to the infant's camp, the noble widow of Hector!

ANDROMACHE falls to her knees for joy.

ANDROMACHE   Oh gods, O Thou of Mercy!

HECUBA kneels with her, as does POLYXENA, and all embrace. KRATOS comes back through the dark entrance and watches them.

HECUBA   They are with us,
They see. Now it begins.

ANDROMACHE   O Thou of Mercy…

POLYXENA   You're going to see your son, Andromache!

TALTHYBIUS helps ANDROMACHE to her feet. She takes a ribbon from him, and he helps her to bind her eyes. HECUBA and POLYXENA rise.

ANDROMACHE   Let go, let go, I can do this, I can do this...

HECUBA   So proud are the gallant Greeks of the world they make
that not a soul may see it.

TALTHYBIUS   Once through the gate
to the infants' cave, your sight shall be restored.

ANDROMACHE   And there will be my son!

TALTHYBIUS   And up we go now…
This man is here to assist you (are you not?) *[KRATOS]*
with preparations for your rehousing,
and the move to the new quarters. He is required
(as he well knows) to help in any way.
I wish you all good morning.

TALTHYBIUS guides ANDROMACHE, blindfolded, out through the light exit. KRATOS, picking up his jug of 'mercy water', looks at HECUBA.

KRATOS   Thirsty, Mother Rat?

HECUBA is but doesn't drink.

POLYXENA *[To KRATOS]*   You are required
to assist with preparations.

KRATOS   Yes I am.

POLYXENA   But you just stand there.

KRATOS   All sorts of ways to help.

Like telling you your fortunes, like *she* does,   *[CASSANDRA]*
the little witch. Only, when *I* do that,
I tell the truth. I'm not your chambermaid.
In my spare time I happen to stand guard
on the Council of the Generals, so I know
a thousand times what *he* knows.   *[TALTHYBIUS]*
Thirsty, little Biter, little Mouse?

POLYXENA drinks.

KRATOS Rehousing. Resettlement. Them quarters
he's prattling on about. He hasn't seen them.
But I've peeked in every window. They're not bedrooms
they're bone-yards. You're going to get your quarters.
They're on our ships. You're coming home with us,
I heard the generals say so, when the wind blows.
It blew last night, it sort of blew, it was something,
it let the secret out. You, come with me.   *[CASSANDRA]*
They want to hear some jokes.

KRATOS leaves through the light exit with CASSANDRA. The drug takes hold.

POLYXENA Mother…

HECUBA   He doesn't know. He is no one.
Pity him, Polyxena, he knows
nothing.

POLYXENA   He is required…to assist…

HECUBA Listen, I will tell you what I dreamed!

POLYXENA *I dream of him I always dream of…*

POLYXENA sleeps.

HECUBA   No!
They actually believe we are defeated.
When I have seen what I have seen these nights!
When the wind blows it will rain on the horizon
and grow a thousand ships like silver corn…

HECUBA drinks.

HECUBA O Thou of Justice, pity these poor Greeks

23

as you abandon them. Let me not be
vicious in triumph nor cruel in victory,
but let your will be done, when the island fleet
appears at the ocean's edge. O Palidorus,
my son, be merciful, your father Priam
is pleading *O be merciful…unto…*
our enemies...

HECUBA *sleeps.*

ACT TWO

A chamber on the surface. AGAMEMNON at a small table, looking at some plans. TALTHYBIUS comes, with his notes. AGAMEMNON doesn't look up.

AGAMEMNON	You're going to tell me that the wind blew, are you.
TALTHYBIUS	Well yes, it did, but also –
AGAMEMNON	That the wind blew,

and the sun rose, that's next on the agenda,
and your wise counsel would be what: keep breathing.

TALTHYBIUS	No, yes, I was going to say –
AGAMEMNON	The wind blew

for the last time on earth, to remind us Greeks
the gods did love us once.

TALTHYBIUS	It will come back.
AGAMEMNON	*You* did. Why did you?
TALTHYBIUS	Matters arising…
AGAMEMNON	Clouds of paper.
TALTHYBIUS	The lady

Andromache and her son Astyanax
are reunited happily.
– You should have seen their meeting. She knew him
from across the dusty camp, she couldn't see him
but she ran to where he was somehow, ran faster
than a champion to clasp him. Every other
infant there was silent.

AGAMEMNON	Finally Troy

has infantry that's worth the name.

TALTHYBIUS	These acts

of mercy, of compassion, they have meaning,
they resonate, they…well.
– General, I was wondering why it was
that she, the Lady Hector, must be brought back
to the cave without her son Astyanax?
Could they not remain together?

AGAMEMNON	Or I could join them,

	play in the sand with them, a happy family,
	couldn't I, make sandcastles perhaps
	but instead I'm stuck here in this hole with you.
TALTHYBIUS	He's a small child.
AGAMEMNON	The widow
	and her *small child* are to be kept apart
	by the vote of the special Council of the Generals
	until some *other* special vote of the special
	fucking special generals. That child,
	to all intents and purposes, *is* Troy.
	He will be raised a *Greek* small child. In time
	she'll have to let him go.
TALTHYBIUS	I understand that.
	In time. I just don't see
	the reason for the blindfold.
AGAMEMNON	You don't *see* it!
	– Never mind.
TALTHYBIUS	Andromache – I got it –
	is an educated woman. She knows
	there's nothing left.
AGAMEMNON	That's education for you,
	knowing there's nothing left. Knowing there's nothing
	is not the same as *seeing* there's nothing, yes?
	They see their town in ruins and they'll screech
	some horror into being. Every day
	they sing when they come out, they hit notes
	there never were, notes between the notes
	we have, they scare the men, and if the men
	look in those deep dark eyes you know the score,
	Talthybius, we get a hive of half-breeds.
TALTHYBIUS	Well. I've another question.
AGAMEMNON	Do you.
TALTHYBIUS	Why is the soldier posted as a guard
	on the cave of the royal captives given license
	to drug them when he likes?
AGAMEMNON	He's not. Does he?

TALTHYBIUS	And stands there in the room they sleep in.
AGAMEMNON	Does he.
TALTHYBIUS	Why can't they be left alone?
AGAMEMNON	Why can't *I* be.
TALTHYBIUS	It doesn't look good to –
AGAMEMNON	Look *good*?
	And who the fuck is looking. You? You're looking?
	And what'll you do about it? Whip a storm up?
	Bring lightning down? Uh-oh, the *gods* are looking?
	Do you feel the wind?
TALTHYBIUS	Well no –
AGAMEMNON	There *is* no wind!
	It – snorted in the night because it couldn't
	hold its laughter in, that we're washed up here
	on a shoreline with these spoilt whining bitches
	for as long as the gods detest us. *Here's* the wind,
	here's some fresh air for you, friend: inform
	the noble ladies they are bound for Greece.
TALTHYBIUS	They're – pardon?
AGAMEMNON	It was settled in the Council.
TALTHYBIUS	We're – taking them? But we're rehousing them,
	in quarters, in new quarters –
AGAMEMNON	Yes, in Athens.
TALTHYBIUS	As – citizens?
AGAMEMNON	Are you out of your mind?
	As slaves. We're drawing lots for them.
TALTHYBIUS	No, no,
	monstrous –
AGAMEMNON	Take it up with Odysseus,
	he'll tell you what you want to hear. Slaves,
	concubines, who knows, *wives* even,
	like I say, it's a lottery.
TALTHYBIUS	The – princesses?
	The queen?
AGAMEMNON	She's not a queen. I'm not a king.
	I'm a king among some kings. Ten weeks ago

we voted all our powers away in favour
of raising hands like children in class.
Me please, me, choose me! Democracy.
Break the news. Those are the ones we're taking.
That list right there. You read it, I can't read it.
We had to use the nicknames, we don't have
squiggles for their noises.

TALTHYBIUS reads.

TALTHYBIUS *Blacklip. Bawler. Biter.*
Sobber. Stripper. Moonface.
Mongrel. Cancan. Dead-Eyes. Mother Rat.
Shell-girl. Slut-of-Sparta.

AGAMEMNON Cross out Slut,
cross out Sparta, cross out –

TALTHYBIUS Helen.

AGAMEMNON Whatever.
That's my brother's business. We voted.
He can screw that up to his heart's content, cross her out.
And cross out the demented one, you know –

TALTHYBIUS Cassandra.

AGAMEMNON You're a dab-hand at the names,
Talthybius. It took me years to manage
yours and it's Greek. How long did it take you?

TALTHYBIUS 'Dead-Eyes' is what they call her.

AGAMEMNON Cross her out,
Tomtibbius.

TALTHYBIUS What happens to Cassandra?

AGAMEMNON You know her name, you ask her.
She can tell her *own* damn fortune. She does that
for the captains, day and night, round the campfire.
Oh the shit she told Odysseus was coming!
He laughed so hard the fire blew out.

TALTHYBIUS This – action
is unconscionable, these women are the royal
House of Troy.

28

AGAMEMNON	The House of Trojan Whores.
	Trojan Whores – like *horse*, but – on we go.
TALTHYBIUS	It wasn't a Trojan horse, it was a Greek horse.
	That's how it will be remembered.
AGAMEMNON	Yes I like that.
	The…Greek…Horse. Remember to write it up.
	After you've told the ladies their fortunes.
	You're good with news, you make catastrophe
	sound like small talk. And there's something else.
	– What?

KRATOS has come.

KRATOS	That Island King.
AGAMEMNON	He's not a king.
KRATOS	He's dressed like one.
AGAMEMNON	Oh pardon me he's a king then.
	I mean, let's all be kings, we'll have a rota.
	Tintabbius here will make a schedule.
KRATOS	Mestor
	of Mestor.
AGAMEMNON	Tell the king to wait outside.
	He can rule his kingdom with a rod of iron
	till we say *You can come in now.*

KRATOS goes.

TALTHYBIUS	That's the man who guards the princesses.
AGAMEMNON	Is it really, write that down, underline it,
	good, now point to it with some little arrows,
	now draw a little boat, oh for fuck's sake
	let it go, Talthybius. Where was I?
	Yes, does one of your ladies sport a bracelet.
TALTHYBIUS	Pardon?
AGAMEMNON	A golden bracelet. Close the door.

TALTHYBIUS goes and comes back.

AGAMEMNON	The Myrmidons…'saw' him again last night.
	I know, I know. Achilles.

He was vaguely near his tomb, they say, some say
beside it, some say *on* it, and some say
he was hovering some inches *over* it,
and he said to them, they say:
Where are you bound, you Greeks,
that you leave my tomb without its gift of honour?
Or some such, but you see where this is going.

TALTHYBIUS   Not quite.

AGAMEMNON   There was this, always this rumour,
that he used to – meet with one of them in the temple.
One of your ladies, *Ratface* or *Dogbreath*
I don't know. 'Reliable' witnesses
of the kind who saw him floating last night
and speaking far more eloquently than ever
he did down here – they say the one he met with
wears a golden bracelet.

TALTHYBIUS   I don't understand –

AGAMEMNON   If it wears a golden bracelet
we won't be drawing lots for it – get it?
It's going to have to die. Like all of us,
only much much sooner.

TALTHYBIUS   You won't grant this,
will you?

AGAMEMNON   Kings, votes, don't get me started.

TALTHYBIUS   They just want blood, the Myrmidons.

AGAMEMNON   Oh I see.
They just want blood. That's why they came to Troy,
abandoning all they loved, do I have that right?
Sweet Mrs Myrmidon in her pretty
myrmidress and their little myrmidaughter
and myrmidog by the fire, they wanted blood
so they left all that behind, did they? Ten years,
ten years in this wilderness with these
primitive fanatics, ten years
to get justice but oh no, all it was was blood,
says wise Talthybius the note-taker.

If *you* see a ghost and tell me what it wants
I'll say fuck you you're lying but if *they* do,
these men, these Myrmidons, then they can *have* that,
for the years they spent and the blood they spilt they can *have* that,
so do I grant? Yes I grant. Golden bracelet.

TALTHYBIUS   You call the Trojans primitive fanatics
but you're going to let this happen. A young girl,
innocent, perhaps about the age –

AGAMEMNON   Of my daughter Iphigenia.
Now that would be a cue for the wind to blow.
That would make me think the gods were bothered.
But nothing. Human nothing. Mortal tick-tock.
Go on. This golden-bracelet girl, perhaps,
is the same age as my daughter was. There. Said it.
Meant to think it, said it. When I was young
I thought things without saying them, you know,
the other way round. I had power.
Now I have things jotted down. Go on.
Go on. I put the love of the gods before
the love of my own flesh, go on, say so.
That I let them kill my daughter for what,
my country, honour, empire, can't remember.
Try to make it hurt. Good luck with that.
Right. Go and do the bidding of Achilles,
as if Achilles cared, or the gods cared,
or I cared. And find me a guardsman's things.
Drugs and dreams and Dead-Eyes…
I'll go and guard these bitches myself.

TALTHYBIUS goes. A gust of wind blows AGAMEMNON's plans off the table.

AGAMEMNON   Fucking hilarious.

KRATOS comes.

KRATOS   The Island King's still waiting.
AGAMEMNON   For what,
the hurricane? He missed it.

MESTOR comes, richly dressed, and sits down opposite AGAMEMNON.

AGAMEMNON	Tell him he is welcome to sit down.
MESTOR	We're sitting down together.
AGAMEMNON	So we are.
[To KRATOS]	Wait outside. Inform the mighty kings
	they can help themselves to olives.

KRATOS goes.

AGAMEMNON	So what's what.
MESTOR	You was busy at your work.
	We was busy at our work.
	And now we sit together.
AGAMEMNON	What's your work,
	polishing your medal?
MESTOR	That's right.
	We do it ourself we do.
AGAMEMNON	Why are you here,
	Mestor, King of Mestor…
MESTOR	True that's me,
	Mestor, and our island is called Mestor.
	When voices say our name they say our island.
	When voices say/ our island –
AGAMEMNON	/I understand the concept,
	Mestor. Why have you come?
MESTOR	We do remember
	the afternoon we two rode on two horses.
	By the Black Lake we rode and spoke of matters.
AGAMEMNON	I'm sure we did.
MESTOR	And we stood and watched the waves.
AGAMEMNON	Right, so a packed schedule. How strange
	it's slipped my mind.
MESTOR	That was the greatest day
	in the history of Mestor.
AGAMEMNON	Oh. It was?
MESTOR	Great in the history
	of Mestor the island, *and*/the history –
AGAMEMNON	/The man, I get it,

	I'm sure it was. And we made an – alliance?
MESTOR	We made a great alliant.
AGAMEMNON	Though you already,
	correct me if I'm wrong, *had* an – *alliant* –
	with Troy?
MESTOR	We had an alliant.
	Now we have two alliants. Two beats one.
	The war is over.
AGAMEMNON	Nothing escapes Mestor
	of Mestor.
MESTOR	True, and all of the great kings
	who fought with you shall have of the great prizes.
	We shall have of the great prizes and our sons
	New Mestor and Small Mestor
	shall have of the small prizes.
AGAMEMNON	You have your medal,
	Mestor, polish it.
MESTOR	We have been told
	there's dicing to be done for the high ladies.
AGAMEMNON	What?
MESTOR	We terrible kings who fought with you
	shall dice for the great prizes of high ladies.
	The Queen there was. The Princess by Fire.
AGAMEMNON	No, no, Mestor, that's internal, that's
	private: Odysseus, Nestor, Ajax,
	Neoptolemus, the boys.
MESTOR	And plus Mestor.
	Odezius, Nector, Ajaps,
	Noptolemy, plus Mestor.
AGAMEMNON	You are an ally,
	for which we're very grateful, friend. Your tiny
	patch of pebbles came in very handy
	for loading and unloading and I clearly
	see you've profited from this already
	but that's it for the great prizes. Farewell.
	Look, you're still here. In our language,

Mestor, we have words that change shape
according to the tense. They decline.
The word *farewell,* for example, in this case,
would be pronounced *fuck off,* it's a steep decline
but what are kings in the face of grammar? – what's that?

MESTOR has produced a silver bracelet.

MESTOR	Silver circle.
AGAMEMNON	I see what it is. What is it?
	This is royal Trojan silver. Where'd you get it?
	Whose is it? Then we'll talk about high ladies.
MESTOR	There was a Prince of Troy and he was hiding
	with Mestor, *on* Mestor.
AGAMEMNON	Palidorus?
MESTOR	His name began with *pal*. Ended with *us*.
AGAMEMNON	Through all this shit he's been hiding out with you?
	A Prince of Troy? I trod on your little rock
	and you didn't say?
MESTOR	We spoke of other matters.
AGAMEMNON	What other matters?
MESTOR	Matters between kings.
AGAMEMNON	You're the king of a fucking paperweight, Mestor,
	what matters more than hiding a Prince of Troy?
MESTOR	It was the greatest day in the history
	of Mestor the man –
AGAMEMNON	Shut up. Where is he now?
	Where is he now?
MESTOR	In his field.
AGAMEMNON	Doing *what* in his field?
MESTOR	Nothing. He got strangled.
AGAMEMNON	When?
MESTOR	When he was eating.
AGAMEMNON	– Right then. Palidorus.
	We thought perhaps he'd come with his island friends.
MESTOR	He got no friends. Not now as he got strangled.
AGAMEMNON	Yes it's amazing how they melt away.

MESTOR	We was in a war with Troy, is why we done it.
	We want a prize.
AGAMEMNON	We'll find you a pal, Mestor.
MESTOR	The Princess by Fire.
AGAMEMNON	No, not a princess.
	We are taking them away with us to Greece,
	you understand? We'll find you
	some bride from the catacombs, we'll clean her up,
	you can make her Queen of Mestor, she can wear
	a pebble necklace you can polish nightly
	as you throttle her, it's your island. Farewell,
	Mestor, and fuck off. Both meanings.
	Show yourself out.

AGAMEMNON goes, taking the bracelet.

KRATOS comes.

MESTOR	Ogenius, Neptune, Jaybat, Solomon, Mestor.
	We Sackers of Great Troy. You are he
	who stands guard by the cave of the high ladies,
	by The Queen and by The Princess by Fire.
KRATOS	What did you say?
MESTOR	They tell us they sleep fast,
	the high ladies, they drink the murky water.
KRATOS	I don't know what you're on about there, chief.

MESTOR piles gold pieces and shoves them one by one towards KRATOS.

MESTOR	They drink the murky water.
KRATOS	So they do,
	they do indeed, high ladies yes, I guard them.
MESTOR	You are he, and we are them who grants you
	this from the stone island. Each coin
	is worth this side and that side, so *two* coins.
KRATOS	You're on both sides, chief. Call: heads or heads?
MESTOR	Yes.
KRATOS	Ri-ight. That's a tower of heads you got me.
MESTOR	Is there a prize there is

who was a Princess only in the old time
and in the new time sits by the night fire
seeing what was never?

KRATOS You mean Dead Eyes.
She's lost her mind, chief, you could do much better.

MESTOR Does she sleep where the prizes sleep?

KRATOS She doesn't sleep.
She lies awake all day.

MESTOR We lie awake
all night.

KRATOS You want some face-to-face with Dead Eyes?

MESTOR stands, thoughtful. He dances to a song of his.

To and fro, to and fro…
She shall have a pebble necklace
And the pebbles shall be rubies
We shall cover her with rubies
And when the night is fire
She shall cool us with her time
And we shall sing our song then
So shall begin the new time

MESTOR dances away, transported. KRATOS pockets the coins, and follows.

ACT THREE

The cave. HECUBA, POLYXENA and CASSANDRA have made blindfolds from their clothes, and are moving in patterns as they sing, mapping out Troy in their minds.

HECUBA	*Where Sundial Gate is found at one*
POLYXENA	*For Crystal Square you make a turn*
HECUBA	*At six there is a lemon grove*
CASSANDRA	*At nine there is a lady's grave*
POLYXENA	*At ten there is a tent of gold*
HECUBA	*There the silk is bought and sold*
POLYXENA	*The trees make patterns on the walls*
CASSANDRA	*At seventeen high waterfalls*
	Are heard again – but are not seen
POLYXENA	*Until – the statues at nineteen!*
HECUBA	*Where the right turn will bring you straight*
POLYXENA	*Down Sugar Street – to Sundial Gate!*

They celebrate having mapped this out, and take off their blindfolds – KRATOS brings ANDROMACHE through the light entrance: she has seen her son is alive. KRATOS watches the dance with suspicion, and withdraws. The WOMEN are joyful.

ANDROMACHE	It's wrong, it's not a right turn it's a left turn.
HECUBA	Coming down the slope it's a right turn.
POLYXENA	From the olive grove it's a left turn!
ANDROMACHE	But of course
	you're coming from the grove, what do we know
	of Polly's private Troy? Nothing at all!
	The cloisters turn the air to green –
POLYX/ANDRO	*Do what you can, you can't be seen!*
ANDROMACHE	You know those lines so well!
POLYXENA	I do by heart!
	Did you see Astyanax?
ANDROMACHE	He's so grown-up
	he didn't even cry, he didn't need to,

	I cried enough for both of us –
HECUBA	Where is he?
ANDROMACHE	I'll see him again soon, the man assured me –
POLYXENA	You'll have to be together for the journey.
ANDROMACHE	He's grown, he's so much taller! …what journey.

POLYXENA puts her hand to her mouth. CASSANDRA puts her arm around ANDROMACHE, who brushes it off. CASSANDRA goes and sits apart.

ANDROMACHE	What journey, Hecuba?
POLYXENA	It's not a secret –
	is it, mother? Was it?
ANDROMACHE	What journey, Hecuba?
HECUBA	Not a secret,
	not a truth, and not a journey.
ANDROMACHE	What journey?
POLYXENA	He told us, him who brought you, who was here
	to assist with preparations. For – a journey.
HECUBA	They threaten us with lies.
ANDROMACHE	You mean – to Greece?
HECUBA	They are terrified, I see it in their faces,
	the sea is flat as gold, they are deserted
	by Those who hold us dear, so they threaten us
	with lies –
ANDROMACHE	What is she saying?
POLYXENA	Yes, to Greece,
	but we're remembering everything, aren't we,
	mother, so we'll build a whole new Troy
	wherever the Greeks might take us.
HECUBA	Troy is here,
	daughter, here.
POLYXENA	We'll build a whole new Troy
	among the Greeks!
ANDROMACHE	My darling is alive,
	we're happy, we'll play hide-and-seek in Hades.

TALTHYBIUS comes through the light entrance.

TALTHYBIUS	Beautiful… I heard you at your dancing.

It's good to be, it's very – to be dancing.

TALTHYBIUS takes out his papers. HECUBA and POLYXENA recoil.

HECUBA	Clouds of evil!
TALTHYBIUS	Yes, my clouds of evil,

very good, poetic, clouds of evil,

a metaphor, they're just this man's reminders.

POLYXENA   What do they say will happen?

TALTHYBIUS   No, princess,

they don't say what will happen quite, they say

what's next in terms of well, the –

HECUBA   Turn them back,

turn them back and find my Priam waking,

my Priam young, our walks by the Scamander,

my Hector in his armour, turn them back

until you never sailed here! Turn them fast

and there's the breeze you want! You will die here

begging us to beg our gods to blow

your bodies home. Turn them, turn the leaves!

TALTHYBIUS   This does not reveal tomorrow, it does not

undo, it does not *do*, what does it do?

nothing, ha! See there, see there?

The pages are all blank, nothing doing,

all the poems I never wrote, white mornings

[+ **CASSANDRA***]* **just like my mind.**

TALTHYBIUS stares at CASSANDRA.

TALTHYBIUS   How did you do that?

[+ **CASSANDRA***]* **How did you know –**

ANDROMACHE   She isn't well. Leave her be. Is it true

you mean to take us with you? And if so,

I need my son with me –

POLYXENA   And the four of us

need to be kept together, Greek gentleman,

we are the Royal House –

HECUBA   And do you mean

to make the sun turn purple and your ships

> grow legs so they can walk the long way home?
> Tell us a story, slave –

TALTHYBIUS *[+ CASSANDRA]* **Leave me alone!**

TALTHYBIUS, beleaguered and freaked out, tries to test CASSANDRA.

TALTHYBIUS   Last night…I dreamt…of *hummingbirds.* There. There.
Nobody could know that, nobody did.
You're in the dark. We're in the dark together.
Ladies, I can only… Ladies.
I will say it now, it will end then, end quickly.
We are taking you to Greece, not all of *them*,
but most of you. There are no, no quarters.
You are to be separated. You are to be chosen
by random lot, determining which person
of higher rank take prior choice, and thereupon
you are to be dispersed and taken forth
from here as spoils of war, as, as, as servants,
as, as, as, as, as slaves. It's written here
in script, I neither wrote this nor chose it,
nor approve of it, I only transcribed it
in my role as, in, in terms of – I was once
a poet, men and ladies sipped wine
and listened to me, I hoped one day to alter
lives, make a mark on lives, and now,
if you look, I do,
I do, I bring them tidings of their ruin
and so, and now we fold it all away
and wait for rain.

Silence then pandemonium, which brings KRATOS and a GUARD running in through the light entrance.

HECUBA   No! No! No!
POLYXENA   He said *separated*!
ANDROMACHE   Take me to my son right now!
HECUBA   O hear us
Thou of Justice! Thou of Blood, strike now!

KRATOS, TALTHYBIUS and the GUARD, after a struggle, manage to bind and blindfold HECUBA and ANDROMACHE. Overlapping cacophony –

HECUBA	You are slaves and liars all, I pity you!
KRATOS	Tell your brand new master, Mother Rat.
ANDROMACHE	Talthybius I will sail if my son sails –
TALTHYBIUS	Rest assured, whatever is in my power…

KRATOS and TALTHYBIUS take HECUBA and ANDROMACHE out through the light exit. POLYXENA tries to go with them, but the GUARD – AGAMEMNON in disguise – firmly holds her back. She sinks down, distraught. He helps her to her feet and sits her on a bed.

GUARD There-there, it's alright, it's alright.

[+ CASSANDRA] **No point in cryin', is there.**

Rest up, get your strength.

[+ CASSANDRA] **You'll see them by and by.** Who's doing that?

CASSANDRA You are. So am I. You are the king
of what gets said.

GUARD What's she talkin' about?
I'm just an humble soldier.

CASSANDRA You are dressed
that way to come among us,
because you think kings do that,
like stories you had read to you,
and so you come, because you're sad
because the ocean's flat and you
can't sail because they hate you.

GUARD So tell me, little seeress, why do they?

CASSANDRA Read the past, you have that power,
if not a pip beyond it, Agamemnon.
That, and watch for scorpions.

AGAMEMNON Really. Scorpions.

[+ CASSANDRA] **Why, is that how I die?**

You did it again. Scorpions…that's my fate?

CASSANDRA Nope.

AGAMEMNON I bet it is. I'm going out
to make a friend of a scorpion, and die

cackling at how wrong you were. Well. Hecuba
and Hecuba. Ye gods, your old mother.
I knew her years ago, you know. She was both
a beauty and a hound-from-hell and look:
a beauty *[POLYXENA]* and a hound-from-hell *[CASS].* The lady
is duplicated. Didn't *you* think I made
a lifelike sort of guard?

POLYXENA   I didn't think
you made a king.

AGAMEMNON   Till now, you mean, till now.

POLYXENA   King, I have a question.

AGAMEMNON   Do you now.

POLYXENA   If we have to go to Greece we have to go,
and live among the warriors, like you,
and the great ones.

AGAMEMNON   I – what?

POLYXENA   I wish to know
which of those men the stories are about
are still alive, or if they're just – in stories.

AGAMEMNON   Well…*some* are just in stories.

CASSANDRA   They're all in stories.

AGAMEMNON   Shut it, you.

POLYXENA   I'm thinking about the greatest
warrior of all!

AGAMEMNON   Are you now.
Give me your hand, little princess.

*AGAMEMNON takes her hand, looks at the bracelet, sees the '**a**'. Their eyes
meet.*

POLYXENA *[a whisper]* He lives? He is alive?

AGAMEMNON   Yes and no.

POLYXENA   Will everyone stop saying that to me!

*She pulls her hand back. AGAMEMNON goes over to CASSANDRA, grabs her,
kisses her, turns her, throws her on the ground and stands over her.*

AGAMEMNON   Did you see *that* coming, did you?

CASSANDRA   Yes and no.

POLYXENA	Lord, please let her be!
CASSANDRA	That's much better,
	much more like a guard. And you can't see me,
	you only see my back, now we'll be lovers
	in the Greek style.
AGAMEMNON	That's right I'm right behind you,
	you'll wonder where I am,
[+ CASSANDRA]	**you'll never see me coming.**
	Tell me how you do that.
CASSANDRA	How I do what.
AGAMEMNON	You say the words I say as if you thought them.
CASSANDRA	Been in the thoughts of men, I know the forest.
	Ask a scorpion why it flies.
AGAMEMNON	It doesn't.
CASSANDRA	Ask it anything, it will still bite you.
AGAMEMNON	Lie there, hound-from-hell, sleep in your forest.

CASSANDRA lies still, at peace. AGAMEMNON goes over to POLYXENA.

AGAMEMNON	So. Pollycasina.
POLYXENA	So. Amaglegnon.
AGAMEMNON	Oh I like that, he sounds powerful,
	King Amaglegnon, All Hail –
POLYXENA	Be quiet,
	king. That man of war, that hero *[she signs 'a']*
	is he hurt, is he in the city –
AGAMEMNON	What city.
POLYXENA	Does he come to the temple as he did?
AGAMEMNON	What temple.
POLYXENA	The Temple of She of Wisdom.
	By the palace, in the Square,
	by the steps, there are ninety-one,
	you can run up there to the top, and then…
	you can see the whole – you can, in the song you can.
	Is he alive, that man?
AGAMEMNON	I had a girl,
	I had a daughter, you know. She went away.

POLYXENA	Oh? That's sad.
AGAMEMNON	I know. She must be somewhere.
	She'd hate me though, and you don't.
POLYXENA	I do hate you.
AGAMEMNON	No you don't.
POLYXENA	I do!
AGAMEMNON	No you don't.
POLYXENA	I curse
	the name of every Greek!
AGAMEMNON	Do you curse Achilles?
	Do you curse him, Pollycasina?

POLYXENA stares at her bracelet.

POLYXENA	You shouldn't have said his name.
AGAMEMNON	I – knew your mother.
	In the old days. There was a dance by a lakeside.
	We were shy, like one another. Forty times
	we danced, rather that than…conversation.
	Achilles died in the fire. We don't know how.
	We think your brother killed him. He died too,
	Paris, we assume so.
	Your brother…killed…the killer…of your brother.
	Neat, that. Been practising that.
POLYXENA	Then…he is gone…
	[she signs 'a'].
AGAMEMNON	Pollycasina.
	Some – stories are not stories at all.
	What I have to say is true and is not true.
	In the night, above his graveside,
	some soldiers saw, at least, they say they saw,
	Achilles. At the graveside of Achilles,
	standing there. They say,
	they say he asked for one he says he loved.
	They say he asked for, well.
POLYXENA	He asked for me.
AGAMEMNON	They say he asked for you.

POLYXENA	Of all the girls
	in all the city.
AGAMEMNON	Yes.
POLYXENA	Of all the girls
	in all the world.
AGAMEMNON	He's come for you, and you,
	you have to go. It's just – you're – you're smiling.
	Is that how a Trojan weeps? You seem – joyful.
	Yet you do understand?
POLYXENA	Yes, I do.
AGAMEMNON	He met with you in the temple, is that true?
	After the death of Hector, he came to find you,
	and you went to find him, *after* he killed your brother,
	after what happened. What does that make you, beauty?
POLYXENA	His.
AGAMEMNON	I suppose it does.
	Beauty…and the hound-from-hell. *[To CASS]* You with us,
	hound-from-hell? You asleep?
	You in a trance?
CASSANDRA	*Why is the blind eye crying*
	when it can't see what was done?
AGAMEMNON	What did she say?
	Why is the blind eye crying? No one's blind,
	no one's crying, your sister here's in *rapture*.
	Do you understand what I'm telling you?
POLYXENA	For a king
	you don't know anything.
AGAMEMNON	Pollycasina,
	I would not let them do this. I am chief
	of all this expedition, but we are Greeks,
	beauty, we are Greeks and Greeks vote,
	Greeks decide what Greeks shall do, it's called
	a system, I would dump it in a moment,
	but what power do I have, look at my wrists,
	chained, chained! Else I would set you free,
	Pollycasina.

POLYXENA   You *are*.

Setting me free.

AGAMEMNON   I am? I'm – setting you free.

POLYXENA   He called for me… from the underworld he called…

AGAMEMNON   Well there's lots of votes in that.

POLYXENA   All the world will know

he chose me, won't they.

AGAMEMNON   When they – lift the veil,

yes.

POLYXENA   Then I have a wish to ask you.

AGAMEMNON   Beauty.

POLYXENA   You say you knew

my mother in the old days, in a dance,

by a lake and you were shy like each other,

and all I wish is that – she not be told this,

so she might think, my mother,

that I marry a noble lord, not a Greek lord,

she wouldn't have a Greek lord for me,

but some great noble lord, and we'll sail away

over the horizon, where her hopes

can come to life. For I think she'd come to death

if she knew – what was to happen.

AGAMEMNON   A noble lord,

not a Greek lord, and over the horizon.

I can do that, Pollycasina, yes. A story,

yours and mine.

POLYXENA   Yes a story,

and also, do you see, it's *not* a story.

I promised. I *was* promised. And I go.

AGAMEMNON   And you go…and you *go*. And you – go.

Like that. Heavenly children. Little Troy.

This is your temple now.

AGAMEMNON stares at her in awe. Then suddenly brisk.

AGAMEMNON   Hound-from-hell, let's go, let's go, I want

a weather forecast better than some bluebeard

prodding a pig's insides.

AGAMEMNON picks up CASSANDRA and carries her away through the light exit.

POLYXENA   A story, not a story…

A story, and not a story…

AGAMEMNON *[from off]* Ow! Scorpion! Did you put that there?

CASSANDRA   No.

AGAMEMNON   Am I going to die?

CASSANDRA   Yes.

AGAMEMNON   No I'm fucking not.

POLYXENA rehearses what she'll say to Hecuba.

POLYXENA   Mother…I am to be wed. The man I wed
is a wise man. The man I wed is a wise man.
He knows this world but lives – on a far-off shore.
He means no harm. But gets what he comes for.
He fears no god or man.
I love my husband, mother.
And I will sail so far
to where he lives and I shall want
for nothing there, for I shall want no more.

She curls up on her bed. Light of sunset. We hear the unearthly humming of the SHADOW-WOMEN.

KRATOS leads HECUBA and ANDROMACHE in through the light entrance, removes their blindfolds. The marks of their new masters have been burnt in their clothes. Hecuba bears 'O' (omicron); Andromache bears 'N' (nun).

HECUBA   Odysseus…Odysseus…

KRATOS   Get used to it.

HECUBA   Odysseus…

KRATOS   I imagine you'll be saying
master to the man.

HECUBA   I imagine
nothing.

KRATOS   Imagine nothing
to your heart's content, Mother Rat, nothing's coming

but your future and your future
got scooped out of a bag. *Your* new master,
Neoptolemus, son of great Achilles
(good luck for you!) Neoptolemus commands you
join his household at first light of dawn
to hear instructions for the homeward voyage.

ANDROMACHE You can tell him I will sail if my son sails.
If not he can have my skull for a figurehead,
see if my good luck holds.

KRATOS Wind'll blow
tomorrow, mark my words.
The king had your old Dead-Eyes read the signs
and she says no wind at all. But she *also* says
one day I'll touch a stone and this ghost-face
will tell me all the news back home
as if I was right there! Like a talking stone!
I love that. Ah, we're going to miss old Dead-Eyes.
I'll get you your night water.
Let the record show: Kratos showed mercy.
If they put me in the record.
If they don't I won't show any.

KRATOS goes out through the light exit.

ANDROMACHE Neoptolemus, son of Achilles,
shatterer of lives. Astyanax
won't live in the house of Hector's murderer.
No. There is one power
left that the living have and the dead have not.
We can cross the border.

HECUBA No. We must be ready.

ANDROMACHE Ready?

HECUBA For the war that is to come.

ANDROMACHE Oh Hecuba.

HECUBA Our warriors in the hills
are watching. At the head of a mighty fleet
I saw my youngest son.

ANDROMACHE   Your youngest son's
your oldest son, it's over.

HECUBA   I was *shown* him,
bracelet of silver!

POLYXENA   Bracelet of gold, mother,
be at peace.

HECUBA   They're coming – hush!

KRATOS returns with the 'mercy water'.

KRATOS   That's right, hush… hush…

The WOMEN drink the water. KRATOS goes through the dark exit to give water to the other women. ANDROMACHE and POLYXENA sleep. Once KRATOS has gone, HECUBA spits out her mouthful of water. She looks in the jug, sniffs it.

HECUBA   Slave-water, end of song, end of singing.
Troy asleep forever, under the ocean…
On the far bank the children played…
Sisters fly the kite they made…
Only the Queen of Troy sings on:
Blue the evening blue the shade…
O Thou of Light, show something…

A thing in there is sipping at me, something
from a dismal place is darting out its tongue
for me, that I should drink now, to the deeps,
to the deeps and never wake… O Thou of Blood
be ready, they will come. Thou of Beauty,
you left us on the night the moon was burning…
Console us, inspire us…
Girls are home from temple choir
Mocking whom they most desire…

KRATOS comes back through the dark entrance and HECUBA closes her eyes. KRATOS looks at her mistrustfully, then goes through the light exit. She opens her eyes.

HECUBA   Thugs rolled the dice for us, we heard them fall

> though we were blind, don't think of it, don't drink it…
> 'O', my name is 'O', that was the ring
> they walked us in, a bell rang, a bell rang,
> they made me spell my name into the darkness:
> It is Hecuba, Hecuba… *Hecuba!*
> My husband… do you hear him? I do.
> *Sip it only, Hecuba, don't drink it.*
> *It is not time to join me. They are coming*
> *They are watching, they are sailing. In your dreams*
> *They will find you, He of Light, She of Beauty,*
> *He of Battle, in your dreams they tell you*
> *what's to come. Drink no more than dream*
> *is asking*, he tells me, he instructs me,
> does my thoughtful Priam, do you hear him,
> gods, do you? I do.

HECUBA sips from the jug, grows sleepy.

HECUBA *The ocean that will bear me to your side*
is old and wide as sleep… I am borne
by my love into the bedroom…

HECUBA sleeps. KRATOS, with a lamp, leads MESTOR into the cave through the light entrance.

KRATOS I give you Troy.

MESTOR Twelve prizes! What's in there?

KRATOS Females, chief, till you can't move for females.

MESTOR The Queen of Troy. All brown. Who are you now?
Where's your purple robe and your gold robe,
The Queen? *Brown*, she says.

MESTOR moves HECUBA'S jaw to make her answer.

MESTOR *I bow to Mestor*
of Mestor, to New Mestor and Small Mestor.
Bow-wow, bow-wow, like a dog!

KRATOS Chief, come on –

MESTOR We are done with the Queen of Troy who is the Queen
of brown. *[To HECUBA]* Where is your daughter, the Queen?

KRATOS	I told you –
MESTOR	Where is the prize?
KRATOS	I told you, chief,

she wanders through the camp, they make her dance,
old Dead-Eyes.

MESTOR Make her dance? We will kill them
if they make her dance. *We* will make her dance.

MESTOR dances his dance.

MESTOR *She shall have a pebble necklace*
And the pebbles shall be rubies
We shall cover her with rubies
And when the night is fire
She shall cool us with her time
And we shall sing our song then
So shall begin the new time...
But this is still the old time.
You can go on that one. *[ANDROMACHE]*
We can go on this one. *[POLYXENA]*

MESTOR moves towards POLYXENA.

KRATOS What you doing, chief?
MESTOR When the prize is here,
the prize is here. When the prize is not, the prize
is this.
KRATOS Chief, chief, these women here
are the royal house, or they were, theirs, Troy's,
I guard them, I'm commanded to guard them.

MESTOR stares at him, processing this. Then he brings more coins out of his bag.

MESTOR Heads or heads, heads or heads –
KRATOS It's not –
I can't believe I'm saying this – it's not
about that, chief, those women in the darkness,
through there, there are great beauties in the darkness,
chief, shall we go taste of the great beauties?

MESTOR	Hm. When the prize is here, the prize is here.
	When the prize is not…
KRATOS	The prize is – through there…

MESTOR grabs the lamp and goes through the dark exit. KRATOS follows.

HECUBA stirs, asleep still but disturbed by the noise. Meanwhile lamplight from the catacombs throws shadows of the WOMEN there molested by MESTOR.

HECUBA	Thou of Blood you speak with my mouth…
	Thou of Beauty dances in purple…
	Hecuba, shy Princess of Phrygia,
	Prince Priam is here below, are you my host,
	I am Hecuba, shy Princess of Phrygia…
	Princess, shall we two walk by the Scamander?
	Prince, I walk there every day. Princess
	I know you do.

MESTOR and KRATOS come out of the dark entrance, with the lamp.

MESTOR	Are you calling us, The Queen?
KRATOS	She's asleep.
	She's talking to her gods.
MESTOR	To her what.
KRATOS	Her gods. She's talking to her gods.

MESTOR, puzzled, looks around.

MESTOR	There's no one here.
KRATOS	She – thinks her gods are here.
MESTOR	There's no one here.
KRATOS	She thinks her gods can hear her.
HECUBA	Thou of Light O show me…
MESTOR	Why is she saying *show me?*
KRATOS	She wants a sign from them. She wants a sign
	that Troy will be avenged. From her gods.

MESTOR considers this, chuckles, then laughs hysterically. KRATOS joins in.

KRATOS	She thinks the gods are *everywhere!*

MESTOR roars with laughter then stops very abruptly.

MESTOR	They are.
	Our gods. They are here now. We can see them.
	You are laughing at our gods.
KRATOS	What, what gods?
MESTOR	You are laughing at our gods.
KRATOS	Chief, come on.
MESTOR	You see them not. We see them *there* and *there*.
KRATOS	*You* – have gods?
MESTOR	We have the only gods
	who *are* gods. The things they want we want.
KRATOS	I know what you want, chief. You want Dead-Eyes.
MESTOR	That's not her name. Her name is… *Kakakandra*.
KRATOS	Sort of, chief.
MESTOR	We want the hand in marriage.
KRATOS	What? You?
MESTOR	We want the hand in marriage.
KRATOS	That doesn't sound like you, chief.
MESTOR	It is not.
KRATOS	I mean not like you to ask.
MESTOR	It is like our gods.
	We have our prizes but the prize we want
	we want so far the gods want it too.
	They are here now and they want the hand in marriage.
	They are standing there and here.
	When you hear her name it's them. *Kakakandra*.
	That was them. You hear our gods, The Queen?
	They want the hand in marriage for King Mestor!
KRATOS	Chief, you need to think. She has her gods.
MESTOR	No!
KRATOS	She has the gods she *thinks* she has.
MESTOR	No. They have been eaten by this time.
KRATOS	*Use* her gods, chief. You can *use* her gods.
	You want her favour? Make a sign of beauty,
	a sign of light, or a sign of blood, you know?
	Make her think her gods are using you
	to show her something.

MESTOR doesn't get it. KRATOS makes it very clear.

KRATOS Make *her* think…*her* gods…are using *you*…
to show *her* something.

MESTOR doesn't get it. KRATOS tries to draw it on the ground.

KRATOS Make *her* think – look I know it's not easy.
For a king – I mean, nothing's easy for a king.
But if you're like a god to her, she'll give you
what you want forever!

MESTOR *Kakakandra.*
That was them. *Be silent!* That was us.

KRATOS You make a lake turn black, that'll make the sailors
think of your own island, that lake
you've got that's black as night. Or you get some crows,
a million crows fly up in a sign like 'M',
or you make great boulders hang in the thin air,
stones – stone island – Mestor –
signs, you get it? Omens, auguries,
signs from the gods all pointing to revenge,
all pointing to King Mestor,
the saviour of Troy, the hammer of the Greeks!
Use her gods. She'll give you anything.

MESTOR We *do* turn water black. We *do* make crows
to fly like that, we *do* make boulders hang there,
but how. We have forgotten.

KRATOS How does it happen?
You know. Gods. *It doesn't need to happen.*
Mother Rat goes stone-blind in the sunshine.
We just need to *say* it happened.

MESTOR *Say* it happened…

KRATOS Language, chief. Always there when you need it.

MESTOR *To and fro… the pebbles shall be rubies…*

KRATOS and MESTOR go to the light exit. MESTOR pushes KRATOS clear of it.

KRATOS What's your problem, chief?

MESTOR The gods go first.

KRATOS	Indeed they do.
MESTOR	There, there.
	Hurry yourselves! There. The gods have gone now.
	All that's left is female.

MESTOR exits, KRATOS follows.

Light of dawn. HECUBA wakes, and prays.

HECUBA	Thou of Light, you left your light with me,
	more was revealed. I dreamed of a hand in marriage…
	Polyxena? Polyxena betrothed…
	Polyxena, to a Greek? That will never be.
	O Thou of Light, show more. I will be patient.
	The rosy dawn was patient. I will be patient.

She rises, and begins to move and sway. From the catacombs, the SHADOW WOMEN can be heard moving, moaning, stamping.

HECUBA	*We stand on your unending shore*
	And ships are near and ships are far
	Our daughter's in her wedding white
	Our son is gazing like a star
	The day is new, the day is bright
	For nothing's over, nothing's old
	What lights the heavens lights the world
	What lights the heavens lights the world
	I stroll out in the morning sun

POLYXENA and ANDROMACHE rise, almost sleepwalking at first.

POLYXENA	*I stroll out in the morning sun*
ANDROMACHE	*My dream will come my dream has gone*
HECUBA	*I'm passing by the Diamond Gate*
POLYXENA	*I'm always early always late*
ANDROMACHE	*I'm walking down Winemakers Street*
HECUBA	*Your silver sandals on your feet*

TALTHYBIUS and KRATOS come through the light entrance. TALTHYBIUS watches with interest, KRATOS with scorn. The dance picks up.

TALTHYBIUS	No harm at all in that. You can hear the lilt,

	that ancient, soulful quality. There's a sweet
	innocence, I insist it be respected.
KRATOS	Well *I'm* respecting it. I'm watching something
	I'll tell my kids about one day.
TALTHYBIUS	Indeed.
	How many do you have?
KRATOS	I don't have any,
	do I, I said *one day.*
HECUBA	*We stand on the unending shore*
	And ships are near and ships are far
	Our son is smiling in the sun
ANDRO/POLYX	*For nothing came and nothing's gone*
HECUBA	*Nothing's over, nothing's old*
	What lights the heavens lights the world
ANDRO/POLYX	*What lights the heavens lights the world*
KRATOS	What ships are near and far? What are they saying?
TALTHYBIUS	Just an old song of theirs. Ladies, thank you –

The dance gets faster. CASSANDRA dances into it.

CASSANDRA	*This is the night before the night*
ANDROMACHE	*Light the light that shines no light*
HECUBA	*Beat the drum that bears no skin*
POLYXENA	*Wind the horn that gives no warning*
HECUBA	*Thou of Horror Thou of Hate*
ANDROMACHE	*Beyond the Alabaster Gate*
CASSANDRA	*One night we met a million Greeks*
POLYXENA	*They waited there a million weeks*
TALTHYBIUS	History, history, ladies, please, enough –
HECUBA	*With tears a-flowing down their cheeks*
ANDROMACHE	*Because a man had bored his wife*
	To death and she had made a life
POLYXENA	*Somewhere better, somewhere sweet*
HECUBA	*And so they sailed their dying fleet*
CASSANDRA	*The ocean like a winding sheet*
HEC/ANDRO	*Nothing but the hours to eat*
POLYXENA	*And when the time was almost gone*

HECUBA	*They came and murdered everyone*
KRATOS	They can't say that!
TALTHYBIUS	It's true.
KRATOS	But they can't *sing* it!
TALTHYBIUS	Ladies, enough, it's time –
KRATOS	We say enough!

The SHADOW-WOMEN add their incoherent, wordless sounds.

ALL WOMEN	*They came and murdered everyone*
HECUBA	*Men and women, girls and boys*
POLYXENA	*They murdered cats*
ANDROMACHE	*They murdered toys*
HECUBA	*They murdered light*
CASSANDRA	*They murdered air*
ALL WOMEN	*And when they'd murdered everywhere*
HEC/ANDRO	*They murdered land they murdered sea*
POL/CASS	*They murdered you they murdered me*

KRATOS draws his sword, and slowly the song peters out under threat of force, but CASSANDRA, oblivious, dances on, seeing things.

CASSANDRA	*There was a world and all it was*
	Was all it was and when I wake
	I see it hanging in the dark
	In green and blue against the black
TALTHYBIUS	Hecuba – lady –
KRATOS	Stop this, Mother Rat –
CASSANDRA	*A thing of dust against the dark*
	I see it hanging in the black
	It made the children cry at table
	Home we never came again

TALTHYBIUS draws a knife and holds it to CASSANDRA's throat, but she sings on.

CASSANDRA	*And every afternoon I sleep*
	And when I wake a crowd I meet
	Of people staring in my eyes
	Who see the living where the dead

Will follow I CAN SEE THEM NOW

She stares out, beyond all of the past, right into our eyes. She faints at the sight. The WOMEN lay her on a bed. TALTHYBIUS, with his notes, approaches HECUBA.

TALTHYBIUS	Very regrettable. I do regret
	my actions there, I can assure all present
	I'm not a man of – I had no intention
	of using any means of – lady, lady, *[HECUBA]*
	if I might speak to you alone.
HECUBA	Alone?
	You are alone.
TALTHYBIUS	I am not – yes I am alone.
	Yes I am alone, and this, one, lone person,
	would like to speak with you about your daughter.
HECUBA	She has no dealings with the world. The gods
	have turned her wits.
TALTHYBIUS	Not that daughter, this one.
POLYXENA	Is it time now?
HECUBA *[To TALTHYBIUS]* Oh blow your clouds away.
	I know. She is betrothed to a noble lord.
TALTHYBIUS	Well yes! At long last, news I needn't break.
HECUBA	It was revealed to me.
POLYXENA	My mother sees
	the world-to-come in dreams. I am betrothed,
	mother, to a lord, not a Greek lord,
	but a lord of the far islands.
HECUBA	O Thou of Beauty!

HECUBA embraces POLYXENA.

TALTHYBIUS	Yes, of course. Far islands. Very good.
	The 'betrothal', yes of course. That time has come now.
HECUBA	Polyxena, my daughter,
	bride of a noble lord. My child in white
	for the honour of our people.
POLYXENA	Would you leave us,
	Greek gentleman? Thank you.

TALTHYBIUS steps back but remains in earshot.

HECUBA   I heard him in my dream, so far away
his gods have other names, tell me about him.

POLYXENA   He's a wise man, he lives on a far shore.
He means no harm, or hurt,
he fears no man at all.

HECUBA   Then he's a strong man?

POLYXENA   His castle is the strongest. No one's ever
conquered it, and no one's hungry there,
mother.

HECUBA   So you'll have all you need?

POLYXENA   I will not
want for anything.

HECUBA   You will have children,
a grandson for your mother and for Troy!

HECUBA draws POLYXENA away from TALTHYBIUS, and whispers.

HECUBA   A New Troy is coming, Palidorus
your brother has set sail, for He of Battle
steels me in my dreams –

POLYXENA   Yes –

HECUBA   She of Justice
wakes me with a vow –

POLYXENA   He's waiting, mother.

HECUBA   Will I see this man?

POLYXENA   One day you'll see him, mother,
and you'll see me too that day, perhaps you'll stay
for good with us in our home on the far island.

HECUBA   You will come home to Troy, to Palidorus,
bracelet of silver!

POLYXENA   Bracelet of gold, enough now,
I have to be made ready.

*POLYXENA goes to CASSANDRA and ANDROMACHE, who dress her in a tattered
white robe and place their last jewels on her. TALTHYBIUS goes to HECUBA.*

TALTHYBIUS   I – wish to register, if I might do so,
my most profound respect for the great – tact

	with which this was arranged.
	Who knows what one would do in such a grave
	circumstance?
HECUBA	We do.
TALTHYBIUS	Yes, I mean…
	I mean, I suppose, I don't.
HECUBA	I should be at the ceremony.
TALTHYBIUS	Indeed,
	the 'ceremony'. Well, it was not thought proper.
	Hope is the gift you've given, a merciful dream
	she can believe in all the way to the end.

HECUBA	The end of what?
TALTHYBIUS	She will not know the truth
	until the veil lifts, on the brink, the steps.
HECUBA	I have never understood a word you say.
TALTHYBIUS	I want to express, as a private man, as a mother's
	son, my sympathy –
HECUBA	It's her wedding day.
	I am her mother. It's her wedding day.
	You think I'm the slave of a dog but I'm a mother
	on a wedding day.

It dawns on TALTHYBIUS that it's HECUBA who's in the dark, not POLYXENA.

TALTHYBIUS	Forget I said a word.
HECUBA	Your sympathy?
	What veil, what truth –
TALTHYBIUS	I forgot myself, forget me!
HECUBA	The veil, the truth, the brink, the steps – *Ai! Ai!*
	A sacrifice! A sacrifice! O! O!

HECUBA sinks down, distraught. The WOMEN go to her.

TALTHYBIUS	She didn't know? She didn't know?
	She is the mother, how can she not know?
	Who told me she didn't know? No one told me!
	Damn you all, I do this in good faith!
	It's not a job there ought to be!

POLYXENA   Mother,
there's not a word not true, the lord I love
is gone from the world, I *want* to be where he is!
If I'm consoled, oh be consoled!

ANDROMACHE   Consoled?
Rip off another veil – her wedding vows
are to the dead Achilles, are they not?
Who else would they do *this* for? The man
who tore my love to cuts of meat. Consoled?
I am, that your paramour lies rotting
and you have a starring role in your own slaughter.

TALTHYBIUS   It's time! *[To ANDROMACHE]* Will *you* go with the girl?

ANDROMACHE   Not I.

POLYXENA   Farewell, Andromache. Farewell, Troy.
I know my brother will save you. Mother – mother?
Bracelet of – bracelet of – mother?

HECUBA does not turn.

POLYXENA   Thou of Beauty hold me. Thou of Memory
set me free. And Thou of Love receive me.

POLYXENA and CASSANDRA embrace. TALTHYBIUS and KRATOS blindfold POLYXENA and bind her hands, and lead her out through the light exit to sacrifice.

ACT FOUR

HECUBA remains on the ground. CASSANDRA and ANDROMACHE where they were. Outside we hear the sounds of the Sacrifice: gongs, drums, invocations, flames, and a huge crowd of soldiers cheering. CASSANDRA's vision overlaps with HECUBA's prayer and ANDROMACHE's anti-prayer.

HECUBA	Thou of Beauty hold her.
	Thou of Memory set her free.
	Thou of Love receive her.
CASSANDRA	*In the cool shade in a lemon grove*
	In the cool shade
HECUBA	Thou of Justice hear us.
	Thou of Wisdom guide us.
CASSANDRA	*In the cool shade in a lemon grove*
	White butterflies in a lemon grove
	In the cool shade
HECUBA	Thou of Battle steel us.
ANDROMACHE	Thou of Itching. Thou of Spiders.
	Thou of Sweat. Thou of Toothache.
CASSANDRA	*In the cool shade in a lemon grove*
	White butterflies on a holy day
	White butterflies in a lemon grove
	In the cool shade
HECUBA	Thou of Mercy spare my son.
ANDROMACHE	Thou of Mercy spare mine first,
	me please, me please, me please,
	change the world to my world.

CASSANDRA comes to ANDROMACHE.

CASSANDRA	*In a cool shade in a lemon grove*
	White butterflies on a holy day
	Two children who are not yet born
	Another love whose hand you hold
	Two children who are not yet born
	On a holy day white butterflies

In a lemon grove in a cool shade

ANDROMACHE   Once upon a time Andromache
was never even born.

TALTHYBIUS comes through the light entrance. HECUBA prays on in silence.

ANDROMACHE   I never thought my heart would race to see *you*.
Take me to my son, is it not time?
Take us aboard the slave-ship, shall we row?
Would you like my son and I to take the oars?
He isn't very strong but he's so willing.
Only get me out of this skull-hall,
this mausoleum lit with guttering hopes
that there are gods and if there are
they're here and if they're here they care
and if they care they care for what we care for –
just take me to my son.
Is it time to see my son?
Is it time to see –

TALTHYBIUS   I can take you to see your son.

ANDROMACHE   You can – take me to see my son.
Your face makes your dead parchment look rich
with life. Why am I sitting down,
I am sitting down
not standing when you say that, not, not
leaping in the air. I am someone else
who is sitting down. Let us – try again. I ask you:
may I see my son now?

TALTHYBIUS   Yes – you may – see him.

ANDROMACHE   Look at me, still here. The dream comes true
and I sit and pass the time. But I can see him?
Will he be glad to see me?
Astyanax? *That's my Astyanax!*
Remember when I screamed that? You took me,
didn't you, you said *escort the widow*
escort the widow of Hector to the camp

of the infants to be with her son. To see him.
You took away the blindfold. *Can you see him?*
And I screamed and ran to him, did I not scream?
I ran through all the children all the babies
and picked him up and flew him round and round
like the sun around the world! You were smiling.
You may not think so now but you were smiling.
So then, at at at that time,
you learned which one he was. I was your teacher,
and you you you you learned – you – didn't know
which one he was so you said I could see him.
So then, you knew.

TALTHYBIUS   Good lady,
I was told to bring you to him –

ANDROMACHE   And you did do,
you you you did do – then you you you knew
which which which child he was and I can see him
I can see him now.

TALTHYBIUS   You can see him, my dear lady
Andromache.

ANDROMACHE   Good lady dear lady
you can see him you can see him, you can
tell me where he is you can tell me
which which which one. Good lady good lady.

*CASSANDRA holds out a hand for ANDROMACHE and slowly leads her through
the light exit. TALTHYBIUS appeals to HECUBA.*

TALTHYBIUS   I didn't know. On your gods I didn't know.

TALTHYBIUS goes through the light exit.

*HECUBA is alone. She tries to rise, but cannot. She stays where she is. We
hear the SHADOW-WOMEN moan and keen.*

HECUBA   On your gods. On your gods.
Thou of. Thou of. Thou of.
Are you there, Thou of Light?
Can you see me, Thou of Light?

Do you know me, Thou of Knowledge?

Did you watch our children die?

Did you cry?

May I?

KRATOS and MESTOR come to the light threshold and see her. As she hears them approach, she sinks to the ground.

MESTOR   The queen of brown is dead and brown.

KRATOS   No, chief.

        She belongs to Odysseus now, if he wants her dead

        he'll let her know.

MESTOR   We want the hand in marriage.

        The gods have said.

KRATOS   I'll get you what you want, chief.

        But I always was afraid of the dark, you know.

        Needed something light, something shiny.

MESTOR doesn't get it.

KRATOS   Something gold or silver, something shiny.

MESTOR doesn't get it.

KRATOS   Give me some more money.

MESTOR pays him more coins.

KRATOS   Think I'm getting a grasp of your language, chief.

MESTOR retreats through the light exit.

KRATOS approaches HECUBA, with the 'mercy' water.

KRATOS   Hi-ho, Mother Rat.

        Got a bed there you can lie on.

        Like it down there, do we.

        Fair enough. You know, if you looked at me

        you'd see I was look, I'm trembling.

        You know what I'm trembling with? Trembling with fear.

        Didn't expect to hear that from a Greek,

        did we? But it's true. It's these signs.

        Signs we're seeing hour by hour, I tell you,

        Mother Rat, we don't know what's portending!

HECUBA buries her face in her hands.

KRATOS   That's what the men are doing, just like you,
account of these signs. Shall I tell you about the signs?
Mother Rat? – Well the first sign
was the water in your sacred pond we use,
you know, with the stone animals – Mother Rat?

HECUBA is shaking. KRATOS takes a blanket off a bed and kneels down beside her.

KRATOS   You leaving us? Don't leave us. It's an order,
from a Greek, eh? chin up now, Mother Rat…

HECUBA slowly responds to his ministrations and rises to be kneeling.

KRATOS   Can't have you leaving us, that leaves me
no one to be guarding.

HECUBA   You – *guard* me…

KRATOS   I guard you, right

HECUBA   What do you guard me from…

KRATOS   From, Mother Rat? From danger.

HECUBA   From the murder
of my sons, and my husband,
from the slaughter of my people do you guard me?

KRATOS   Mother Rat…

HECUBA   From my little girl destroyed
do you guard me?

KRATOS   Mother Rat I do my damnesdest
but all them things are gone now, Mother Mouse
I ought to say, you've never done me harm.

HECUBA   So tell me, guard, guard in his mercy, what signs?

KRATOS   Signs, old Mother?

HECUBA   Signs, signs you say,
You say your hand is trembling but it's not.

KRATOS   No, well no, there were – there were no signs,
Mother Rat, it's just chatter, have a drink eh –

HECUBA knocks the water out of his hand, and gets to her feet.

HECUBA   Tell me about your daughters.

KRATOS	Beg pardon?
HECUBA	Tell me about your daughters.
KRATOS	Don't have them,
	don't have sons, don't have children.
HECUBA	Create them.
	Cherish them. Remember them.
KRATOS	There's no one!
HECUBA	I can see them.
KRATOS	No you can't, no one can do.
HECUBA	See them playing.
KRATOS	I say no, not if *I* can't.
HECUBA	They are lovely.
KRATOS	No – *I* see them, *I* see them.
HECUBA	How many?
KRATOS	I – dunno. Four. Five.
HECUBA	Five. What are their names?
KRATOS	Their names?
HECUBA	Their names!
KRATOS	They're – I dunno, not real,
	five lovely girls they are –
HECUBA	Did they marry well?
KRATOS	Eh? That's a bit quick –
HECUBA	Love them, do they love you?
KRATOS	I think so, yes, of course, in their own ways
	they love me –
HECUBA	Hang them all.
	Hang four of them and leave one survivor.
	Which girl survives?
KRATOS	I can't choose one!
HECUBA	Choose one!
	Now turn her mind to sand.
KRATOS	No – not that one!
	…This is no game to play.
HECUBA	Is she better now?
KRATOS	She's better now – there's no one!
HECUBA	How many sons?

KRATOS	Leave me alone, Mother Rat.
HECUBA	You have no sons?
	Oh so you've only girls.
KRATOS	*Course* I got sons,
	four lads, four men –
HECUBA	Their names?
KRATOS	They don't have names!
HECUBA	You don't know their names?
KRATOS	Kratos, Alexandros,
	Milos, Petras –
HECUBA	Slash them all to slivers.
KRATOS	My lads – no way!
HECUBA	No mercy, you can hear them
	sob for mercy, listen for a while
	like we listen out for birds, then just slit them,
	throat by bobbing throat.
KRATOS	Not listening.
HECUBA	One by one.
KRATOS	Fuck you.
HECUBA	*Help me, father*
	they cry and you say *fuck you.*
KRATOS	Can't hear.
HECUBA	*O help me daddy!* No, it's late, it's lights out,
	no more stories now, snuff the candles,
	bedside to bedside go, there's no survivor,
	are they dead now or still kicking, are they dead now
	or bleating for their mummy?

KRATOS breaks away from her.

KRATOS	There's no mummy,
	she's not there, she's not there!
	She don't exist, I mean they don't exist,
	they never did so I won't mourn them murders.
	Is this what you do, this what you did in Troy,
	lie to your mind?
HECUBA	What I describe was done

to everything I loved while it was begging.
Done by you.

KRATOS Not me, I wasn't there.

HECUBA Done by your sons and grandsons.

KRATOS No such persons.

HECUBA Done in your name.

KRATOS What *is* my name, Mother Rat?
Your mind is full of holes, let me fill 'em in.
– Signs were seen, did I say? Your sacred pond
we do our business in, it went from green
to black in the blink of an eye, it went as black
as the lake on the isle of *Mestor*. What a marvel
it was to behold. Then up on the hills we saw
about a thousand crows there must have been,
and they made the shape of this *[m]* like *muh*, you know?
When they flew aloft that form was on the sky,
it was monstrous to observe it, it stayed there.
And then there was them *stones*, stones in the air
like they were birds themselves but no eyes,
no wings no legs no feathers, only stones
set there like they're falling but they stopped!
Them Myrmidons they ain't afraid of shit
but they're shaking like the leaves and there's no wind!
How about that, Mother Rat? Is that the gods
doing the stuff you do, eh?

KRATOS goes through the light exit, passing MESTOR who starts to take out coins. KRATOS ignores him and goes. HECUBA sways and starts to dance, unaware of MESTOR.

HECUBA *A lake gone black as anywhere…*
A thousand crows that mould and mean…
Stones that tremble in the air…
Something shown, something seen…

HECUBA sees MESTOR but doesn't know who he is.

HECUBA Are you a Greek? Only Greeks come here.
And I'm all they leave behind. If you kill me

I'll still be left behind. Kill what's left
and I'm what's left. Who are you?

To her astonishment, MESTOR bows to her.

HECUBA   Whom do you bow to, warrior?

MESTOR   The mother.

HECUBA   The mother of the dead.

MESTOR   We want the hand.

HECUBA   You want what hand, my hand?

MESTOR   We want the hand
in marriage of the Princess by Fire.

HECUBA   The hand of whom?

MESTOR   The hand of whom. *Kakandra.*
That was them gods, excuse them gods, the mother.
The gods say we must ask the mother's hand.

HECUBA   Cassandra? But her mind is gone.

MESTOR   The fire
was in the firelight making her face dark
and light and dark and light. The eyes of her
are dark as a lake and light as a lake. My island's
got a lake so dark we can see our self
seeing our self.

HECUBA   The Black Lake. You are *Mestor.*

MESTOR   The gods say yes.

HECUBA   The water turned to black…

MESTOR   The gods say yes.

HECUBA   The birds make your name…

MESTOR   The gods say yes.

HECUBA   Stones stopping in thin air…
The gods are all around you!

HECUBA kneels before him.

MESTOR   The stone gods,
there, there, here, and in that corner
the stone gods.

HECUBA   My son, my son is with you!

MESTOR   Who. Where.

HECUBA	He's with you on your island! You are Mestor, the beloved friend of Troy! My husband Priam sent our son to you ten years ago when he was small, he sailed with his servants in a longboat to your island, Palidorus, waving his tiny hand with the sunlight on his silver bracelet…
MESTOR	Silver, gold, a ruby, diamonds, a great day in the history of Mestor and of Mestor.
HECUBA	Sacks of gold were sent for safekeeping to your island…
MESTOR	They are safe, they are keeping. There was gold like this gold, diamonds like these diamonds, emeralds like emeralds like these are.
HECUBA	He is safe!
MESTOR	He is safe and he is keeping.
HECUBA	In your palace?
MESTOR	Yes in the marble palace made of marble.
HECUBA	When does he sail for Troy?
MESTOR	Troy. Yes.
HECUBA	When does he sail for Troy?
MESTOR	Now. He does that now.
HECUBA	The gods be praised! How many ships in the fleet? How many ships are sailing?
MESTOR	Sailing ships.
HECUBA	In the island fleet how many?
MESTOR	It is so many it is twelve.
HECUBA	Twelve – hundred ships?
MESTOR	No. Yes. No. Twelve and twelve.
HECUBA	Twelve and twelve? You mean – twelve *times* twelve?
MESTOR	Twelve times *times* twelve!
HECUBA	And the Greeks, the Greeks,

                        they think you are their friend?

MESTOR   Abysseus,
Reptile, Paybacks, Ottoman, Agamomon
think we are their friend.

HECUBA   But you are *Troy's* friend,
the gods know, you are Troy's!

MESTOR   We had two alliants.
Now we have one alliant.

HECUBA   Palidorus,
is he tall now, is he fair now?

MESTOR   Who. Yes.
He is sailing.

HECUBA   Yes, I saw him in my dreams!
He is the last of Troy, he is the first
of what's to come. The infant had to die
to clear the path for him, I see it now,
O Thou of Light, dark are your winding ways
to the dazzling horizon!

MESTOR   Dark and light,
we want the soft hand now.

HECUBA   She shall be yours.
And Palidorus leads them?

MESTOR   She shall cool us
with her time in the new time. A pebble necklace
shall she wear.

HECUBA   My Palidorus leads them?

MESTOR Who. Yes.

HECUBA   At the prow! Prince Palidorus,
King Palidorus of New Troy!

MESTOR   King Mestor
of New Troy, we will be Troy, King Troy,
so our name is Troy and our land is named Troy.

HECUBA When will the fleet appear?

MESTOR   In new time.

HECUBA In – no time? You mean soon?

MESTOR   Yes in no time.

HECUBA	I must be ready!
MESTOR	We go now, the mother.
	We go to take the soft hand in marriage.
	We have twelve gods. Seven gods go with us.
	We leave you the other – two.

TALTHYBIUS comes through the light exit as MESTOR is leaving.

TALTHYBIUS	You need to be ready, Hecuba. What did *he* want?
HECUBA	What *I* want. We *are* ready!
TALTHYBIUS	This is chaos.
	Look – I've two – last things.
HECUBA	Your last things,
	enjoy your last things then!
TALTHYBIUS	Andromache
	has married Neoptolemus.
HECUBA	Of course.
	She lost her husband, so she took a new one.
	I lost my children, may I do the same?
TALTHYBIUS	Well. Her little boy
	was buried where the temple was. So ends
	the line of Troy.
HECUBA	So ends the line of Hector.
TALTHYBIUS	Indeed, alas.
HECUBA	Do you see two stone figures
	standing by you?
TALTHYBIUS	No I confess I don't.
	I see the gifted peoples of the earth
	gibbering at phantoms and I wonder
[+ CASSANDRA]	**when we will all think straight.**

CASSANDRA comes through the light entrance, followed by AGAMEMNON.

TALTHYBIUS	I won't miss *you* when I'm gone.
AGAMEMNON	Look here, Catfish,
	your mother. Stay with her. She needs you.
	You can go wherever she goes.
TALTHYBIUS	General:
	Odysseus made it clear he has no need

for two of them in Ithaca.

AGAMEMNON Make it clear
to him I have no need to give a dog-shit
what needs he has. No one wants this one   *[CASSANDRA]*
so either she goes to Ithaca with *her*   *[HECUBA]*
or she dwells here in the ruins, she can tell
the sun its fortune, she can tell the tides
if they're high they'll be low soon
and if they're low high soon.
They'll pay her shells and seaweed. Hecuba.
Good evening there, old girl.
I say good evening. *[To TALTHYBIUS]* See this lady here?
A treasure of the old world, not your world,
a beauty in the old days. Correction,
a beauty now, these days. And what a dancer.
What a mover. And her illustrious daughter
was a credit to her. Her name was Pollycasina.

TALTHYBIUS Um. Polyxena. Majesty.
AGAMEMNON No, Pollycasina.
TALTHYBIUS *No*. She was Polyxena.
AGAMEMNON Really.
Maybe I'll forget her then. You know,
why don't you write it down, that's what you do do,
isn't it? But let me ask you something,
Talfibbius, Toltibbius, Tintabbius,
who the fuck will *know* how they ever said it?
Write down how she died. It was an example,
it was – you're the writer, make it true in squiggles.
Go somewhere cold and write it.
TALTHYBIUS But – the fleet –
this list –
AGAMEMNON Stuff the list, stuff the fleet,
stuff Greece. Write down the death of what's-her-name
so nobody forgets it.

TALTHYBIUS goes through the light exit.

AGAMEMNON *[To CASSANDRA]* You,
hound-from-hell, don't move.

[To HECUBA] You're very quiet, old girl. You're like the ocean.
Do you know something we don't? Have you got the ear
of Poseidon these days? *We* don't. Sorry old girl,
you don't name them, do you. I should know that:
you told me at that dance, by the lakeside,
remember? You said *Please not to swear,*
prince. And all that afternoon I didn't,
I promise you. Done nothing much but swearing
since, mind you. Which is why the gods all hate me.
You got a little plan going, old girl?
Got friends in highest places?

HECUBA If you want
the wind to blow then do what you did last time.

AGAMEMNON It speaks, it speaks.

HECUBA If you want the fleet to sail,
then do what you did last time.

AGAMEMNON Hecuba,
listen…

HECUBA If you want us to be slaves
then do what you did last time.

AGAMEMNON Ah, you mean
have my daughter murdered. You know what,
I'd completely forgotten that until you said it,
Hecuba, quite slipped my mind, perhaps
I'll tie a knot in my throat, then I'll remember.

HECUBA *Iphigenia.*

AGAMEMNON Oh was that her name?
Damned if I remember, why would I?

HECUBA *Iphigenia.*

AGAMEMNON Got it the first time.

HECUBA *Iphigenia.*

AGAMEMNON Yes why not say it *for* me,
moment to moment. Then again the ocean
has that job already. I have something.

Something I have to give you.

HECUBA   You have nothing.

I have something. Something my daughter gave me.
Words she said.

AGAMEMNON   I don't want them. What are they?

HECUBA   Last words, like any words. *I am gone away*
to a far shore, where there is no harm or hurt,
no fear of gods or men. I am gone there.
No one is hungry there. I will not want
for anything, for I am happy there.
You shall visit me one day.

AGAMEMNON weeps.

HECUBA   There-there, lord of the world,
did you let a pony through your city gates?
My gift of little words you don't believe
has put you to the sword.

AGAMEMNON   By Athena,
look at me, look at me…

HECUBA   *Please not to swear,*
prince. It's the shy beauty of Phrygia
asks that favour.

AGAMEMNON   Oh you temple-dwellers,
you cave-rats, you pitiless lost cause.
You showed us, didn't you. You forty shadows
snivelling in a hollow, that's the last time
we'll pick a bone with you. You proud slaves
to men whose pride is only to own slaves,
I think you made your point. A cordial hour
in sunlight could have settled it, your Paris,
our Helen – idiot: slut, slut: idiot –
exchange, apology, a dance, but no,
not what They had in mind. Who had in mind?
Who had in mind? You never say their names.
I never feel their breath. I feel *her* breath,   *[CASSANDRA]*
your daughter's, I feel *her* breath, like the last

76

breath of – what was here, who you were.
It's the only breath I hear.

AGAMEMNON pulls himself together, decisive.

AGAMEMNON Said I had something for you. A surprise.
I'm getting you out of here. Both of you.
We'll smuggle you down the coast to the marshlands.
You can take some gold.

HECUBA I've everything I need,
Agamemnon.

AGAMEMNON No.
I'm offering you freedom. I am a king
in my spare time, there'll be no vote on this,
no special council. I, Agamemnon,
am offering you freedom.

HECUBA I am staying
here in Troy where Troy is, and my husband,
and what's to come.

AGAMEMNON You can't, old girl, you belong
to Odysseus. Do you know what I heard him say?
I heard him say he didn't want a young one.
He didn't want to fall into temptation
and accidentally spawn a thing of half-blood.
He didn't need a new wife or mistress.
He drew first choice. He said I'll take the queen.
I need a crone to wipe my boots, he goes.
Someone to sweep the coast clean,
someone to mop the ocean up. They're drinking
as I tell you this, Odysseus and his captains,
making an afterlife of eternal chores
for you.

CASSANDRA You'll never do them.

AGAMEMNON That's right,
I'm going to set you free.

CASSANDRA That's not the reason,
Scorpion…

AGAMEMNON	Just ask me for your freedom.
CASSANDRA	…Odysseus won't see Ithaca for years.
AGAMEMNON	Who asked you, Catfish? Go, say your goodbyes.

CASSANDRA goes through the dark exit.

AGAMEMNON By the time Odysseus wakes up you'll be gone.
By the time he sobers up you'll be out of reach.
He won't come looking for you, all he wants
is home.

HECUBA That's all I want. There is a time
you do not know is coming.

AGAMEMNON Hecuba listen:
I'll send with you some men I trust, they'll find you
land along the coast, you'll have a servant,
you'll be provided for, you'll be watched over,
you'll be defended.

HECUBA We need no defending.
There is a time you do not know is coming.

AGAMEMNON Come on girl, think. *She'll* be with you, her,
Cassandra, she'll be there,
she'll tell you stories, try and stop the witch,
she'll make the time pass. You can walk the shore,
swim in the sea, make little Troys of sand,
ye gods, is this not kindly of this gentleman?
No? No? No?

HECUBA There is a time
you do not know is coming.

AGAMEMNON Nothing is coming,
Hecuba, shy princess of Phrygia.
The gods are done with us. They left us something.
A present.

AGAMEMNON places the silver bracelet of Palidorus beside HECUBA.

HECUBA *Mestor…Mestor…*

AGAMEMNON Mestor of Mestor.

AGAMEMNON places the golden bracelet of Polyxena beside HECUBA.

AGAMEMNON	Two presents.
	Sun and moon, eh. Feels like time turned round.
	Now it's the young it's hungry for. It leaves us
	old orphans still here waiting. This is like
	the lakeside. We were shy.

HECUBA rises, unsteadily, and starts to sway in an echo of dance. AGAMEMNON rises and dances with her, in the silence. Suddenly, she pushes him away.

HECUBA	Apollo…Aphrodite…Ares…
AGAMEMNON	Princess we never say them, remember?
HECUBA	Apollo, Aphrodite, Ares…
	Remember? Remember? Thou of? Thou of?
	Thou of dancing thou of fucking
	thou of noise and thou of nothing
	show me nothing show me –
AGAMEMNON	Hush now, hush…
HECUBA	*Hush hush hush hush hushhhhhhhh.*
AGAMEMNON	Hecuba –
HECUBA	*Hush…*
AGAMEMNON	Time's running out –
HECUBA	*Hush hush…*
AGAMEMNON	Odysseus –
HECUBA	*O, O…*
	Hush O hush O hush O…
	Wish wish wish. A wish.
	I have a wish.
AGAMEMNON	What did you say?
HECUBA	I have a wish now, king.
AGAMEMNON	Look anything
	but we need to move, you and your daughter need
	to leave by dawn.
HECUBA	It is not my wish to leave.
AGAMEMNON	You have to leave. Odysseus will find you,
	he's made his boast to everyone, he has to
	do it now, he has to take you with him.

Cassandra won't be going, no one wants her,
she's staying here. If you want to keep Cassandra
you have to take my offer. Leave. Now.
You're no one, you have nothing, and you're free,
so go, go free!

HECUBA   It is not the wish of O.

AGAMEMNON Not the *wish*?

HECUBA   I am O, I am O,
it's the mouth of a well, you know,
it goes to hell, you know. What O desires
is to look in the eyes of the king of the stone island.

AGAMEMNON No no you don't.

HECUBA   It's the last wish of O.

AGAMEMNON Old girl, I said I'm granting you a wish.
I didn't say you could choose it.

HECUBA   O desires
the head of the island king.

AGAMEMNON   Hecuba, look,
we'll chain the monster up, I'll give the order,
I'll have the soldiers teach a moral lesson
and then we'll mop him up and have him exiled.
But I can't try him for murdering a Trojan,
can I? How will that look. He's our ally

HECUBA He was the friend of O.

AGAMEMNON   Indeed he was,
but then you lost, remember. All those islands
are Greek, they don't look Greek but they are Greek.
Wish to god they were *Greece*.

HECUBA   You're king of all,
you can allow my wish.

AGAMEMNON   I'm king of all
and I don't wish to.

HECUBA   Leave me to die then.

AGAMEMNON I don't want you to die.

HECUBA   You wanted those
I loved to die, and it was done. I want

to see the man who slew my youngest son
and my oldest son and my only son.

AGAMEMNON   Old girl,
you're past your prime, what will you do to him,
berate the man to death?

HECUBA   The Trojan women
lie in the further cave. They are the imprints
bodies used to make, the shadows wear
what's left of who they were and they grow spikes
where fingers grew. Can you see them?

AGAMEMNON See them, I can smell them. That'd kill him.
But *freedom*, Hecuba, *freedom*…
the sea you know, the sand you were a child on,
the same horizon…Troy! There'll be a city
here again one day, we'll make it stronger,
Hecuba, you shall dwell there in a palace,
some great house. You'll have your daughter with you
for company, instead of silence *nonsense*,
but, old girl, go in peace.

HECUBA   Oh now the gods
come close to hear the joke: a Greek decides
it's time for peace.

AGAMEMNON   Of course you wish his death.
He should be made an island in his own
blood, but no more bodies, Hecuba.
Ten years, *ten years.* I'm from a place, you know.
A place is missing me. One wish, one wish.
Yours I mean, not mine. You know mine.

CASSANDRA comes in through the dark entrance.

AGAMEMNON Tell her, Catfish, will you?
CASSANDRA There's no point.
AGAMEMNON   Some daughter you are.
That moron Mestor strangled your own brother.
So I'm trying to free you both, only your mother
would rather trade a life of liberty

for a little bout of murder in the dark.

– Sorry am I boring you?

CASSANDRA   You are, yes,

as I know all this.

AGAMEMNON   Oh, listening at the door,

were we?

CASSANDRA   No.

AGAMEMNON   Nosy, *and* a liar.

[To HECUBA] How do you cope with her?

CASSANDRA   She doesn't listen.

[To AGAMEMNON] That's how *you* cope with me. Nobody listens.

I wish to sail away with you and with you

watch the ocean waves.

AGAMEMNON *[To HECUBA]*   So it's Ithaca…

CASSANDRA *[To no one]* (See. Nobody listens.)

AGAMEMNON   …Washing the steps

for Odysseus. Wiping his boots. Chucking out slops.

Remember me, then, when your wringing hands

are clogged in a bucket, remember that your old friend

begged you to go free.

Look at me, old thing, old dancing thing,

meet my eyes and tell me,

is this what you truly want?

HECUBA Tell Mestor I consent

to his marrying Cassandra.

He must come here if he wants her.

AGAMEMNON   *Mestor* wants her?

He asked you for Cassandra?

HECUBA   He did.

AGAMEMNON He can't have her!

HECUBA   I know that. It's a trick,

Agamemnon.

AGAMEMNON   Ri-ight. Yes. Of course.

I knew that.

HECUBA   I should like so much to meet

his children, are they with him?

AGAMEMNON	Hecuba,
	don't do this.
HECUBA	Killer of infant begs for mercy.
AGAMEMNON	Come on old girl, you don't mean Hector's boy,
	I abstained on that.
HECUBA	He must bring both those children
	upon whose heads he swore fidelity
	to Troy.
AGAMEMNON	Hecuba.
HECUBA	You are the king of Greece,
	you can make him do that.
AGAMEMNON	I am the king of Greece
	but I can't save you if you do this, Hecuba,
	I can't save you from Ithaca.
HECUBA	I am O,
	I am queen of what I wish.
AGAMEMNON	You're the slave of it.
HECUBA	We are all the slaves of that, King Agamemnon.
	When we can't speak we dance.
AGAMEMNON	Right. I'll beat the drum, you row the boat.
	But if anything is witnessed I assure you
	we never had this talk. Either way
	you belong to Odysseus now. You have no idea
	how galling this all is. *[To CASSANDRA]* And you:
	be careful.
CASSANDRA	Why?
AGAMEMNON	So you're still here tomorrow.
CASSANDRA	What's tomorrow?
AGAMEMNON	The day we set sail,
	you and I, forever.

CASSANDRA [+ AGAMEMNON] What's forever?

AGAMEMNON	Ha! Knew you were going to say that.

AGAMEMNON goes through the light exit.

ACT FIVE

Darkness. Then light on HECUBA *and* CASSANDRA *dancing. Lamplight from the catacombs shows the shadows of the* WOMEN *echoing their movements.* TWO CHILDREN *have come among them.*

HECUBA
Prepare, prepare, the gods are going
To throw a little birthday party!
Don't prepare, the gods don't care
And winds can blow themselves-o.
Prepare, prepare, a mortal's coming,
Every mortal knows we love him
Don't prepare, we are not there,
And fire can burn itself-o.
Prepare, prepare, O little children
For the ending of this singsong!
Don't prepare, no one's singing,
No one's there, there-there-o.
Little Cassie, Little Cass,
Today is the mortals' birthday treat.
I baked some cakes.

CASSANDRA
I lit the candles.

HECUBA
You licked the plate!

CASSANDRA
Who'll blow the candles
Out? And when's my birthday party?

HECUBA
Tomorrow, Little Cass.

CASSANDRA
My birthday's
Always coming always going,
Gone and to-come and I lick the plate,
Gone and to-come and we blow the candles
Out!

HECUBA
Where will the children go?

CASSANDRA
To the children's room.

HECUBA
Out there to the special
Children's place.

CASSANDRA
To the children's table.

HECUBA	*The children's table. Tell the good ladies*
	Children are coming.
CASSANDRA	*Two children are coming,*
	Two cups, two cloths, two knives, two bowls.
HECUBA	*I hear them coming.*
CASSANDRA	*I hear them going.*
HECUBA	*Tell the ladies, take the children*
	Out to the children's table, it's time
	To care for the children, and say to the ladies
	Bring to the table your beautiful brooches
	Pinned to the beautiful frocks you wore
	To the end of the world. For the gods of stone
	Have company coming!

CASSANDRA goes through the dark exit. MESTOR comes through the light entrance.

MESTOR	There's a bright table there, with all the light
	and not the dark!
HECUBA	And all the dark
	that lights the light.
MESTOR	To and fro! Where is she
	the Queen of Mestor.
HECUBA	Queen of Troy, New Troy.
MESTOR	Who. Yes.
HECUBA	She's in the catacomb.
MESTOR	Why.
HECUBA	She's putting on her bridal veil.
MESTOR	Why.
HECUBA	So you can't see her.
MESTOR	We want to see her.
HECUBA	Why.
MESTOR	It's what the gods want.
HECUBA	What gods.
MESTOR	Him. Them. And that one.
HECUBA	It is bad luck
	to see her now.

MESTOR	We can't see her now.
HECUBA	Yes, you can't see her now.
MESTOR	Our gods can see her!

They see her by the fire
that's dark and light and coming in the past time,
and we see her by the lake that's light and dark
and that was in the new time, we did swim then
and dry ourselves our feet in the black water
for we knew her all her life and met her never.
The pebbles shall be rubies.

HECUBA   And you've brought
your lovely children.

MESTOR   Brought my little piglets.

HECUBA   May I see them?

MESTOR   No they're eating.
Twelve ladies sat them down in there. You can see them
when they're done.

HECUBA   I'll see them when they're done.
And soon I'll see my little boy too.
Palidorus *my* son, your friend,
I'll see him, when the fleet
appears on the horizon, the first ship
we see will be his ship. The men of Greece
will tremble at the sight. Will you be there?

MESTOR   Yes. We have the power of there and here.

CASSANDRA comes from the dark entrance, veiled. MESTOR is transfixed.

MESTOR   *Kakakakandra.* That was the gods like children.
(Be silent.) We had a bride
more true than is the real world and the god world
and we stop time right here.

HECUBA   Now, Little Cass,
how are the little princes?

MESTOR   How are the little thieves.

CASSANDRA   They're very quiet.

MESTOR   It's not like them so much. Were they fighting?

CASSANDRA	Not for long.
MESTOR	They eating?
CASSANDRA	Not any more.

MESTOR *[+ CASS]* **They'll sleep now.**

CASSANDRA goes back through the dark exit.

MESTOR	The bride has said the same thing we say.
	See eye to eye, that means. The sign is good.
HECUBA	My youngest son is happy for his sister.
MESTOR	Who is happy. What sister.
HECUBA	Shall we ask him?
	Are you happy for your sister, Palidorus?

HECUBA addresses thin air. MESTOR follows her gaze.

MESTOR	Who are you talking to.
HECUBA	The boy over there.

MESTOR looks again.

MESTOR	Who are you talking to.
HECUBA	The boy over there.

MESTOR goes over to the space and finds the silver bracelet.

MESTOR	We don't see any boy. We see his bracelet.
	(The gods say it's his bracelet, we don't know that.)
HECUBA	You don't see his wrist inside it? I do.
	We Trojans, we can see the ones we love
	forever by our sides. Your bride to be
	says all the world will see like that one day.
MESTOR	The bride to be is a liar and we love that.
	We've been it. We don't see a boy.
HECUBA	Are you blind?
MESTOR	No. We see a boy. We see what you see.
HECUBA	He's smiling at you.
MESTOR	Not at you at me.
HECUBA	Feast your eyes on him and all the world.
	It's time to go to Cassandra.
MESTOR	Time stood up
	and said so. Where's her room.

HECUBA That one. She waits for you. She keeps it dark.

MESTOR We like it dark.

HECUBA We're glad you like it dark.

MESTOR goes through the dark exit. HECUBA waits, then follows.

AGAMEMNON comes through the light exit with TALTHYBIUS and KRATOS.

AGAMEMNON *[to KRATOS]* The wind blew, we're leaving. Where are they?

KRATOS Through there.

TALTHYBIUS In the catacombs.

AGAMEMNON *[to TALTHYBIUS]* And where are you?

TALTHYBIUS Gereral, please –

AGAMEMNON Where *are* you? Are you here?

KRATOS Come on, Secretary...

TALTHYBIUS No – I'm not here.

KRATOS I'm not here either, sir.

AGAMEMNON Why would we be?

KRATOS Why would we?

TALTHYBIUS This, this man shoud be on trial, *[MESTOR]*
Agamemnon, *he* may be a savage,
but we're not savages, we are the Greeks
and this this this is chaos!

AGAMEMNON What's that noise?

KRATOS Dunno, sir.

AGAMEMNON It was just the wind. Where are they?

Sounds of a scuffle, a commotion in the catacombs.

AGAMEMNON That must be sunrise now. *[To TALTHYBIUS]* Write it down.
and then the sun rose. We can't wait till dawn
for these fucking harpies. How long can it take?

We hear a long animal scream from MESTOR.

AGAMEMNON Talthybius, note, on our way across the bay,
one of the smaller ships will make landfall
on Mestor – are you listening? Are you here?

TALTHYBIUS I'm not here.

AGAMEMNON But are you listening? Where was I...

TALTHYBIUS Landfall on Mestor.

AGAMEMNON	Yes, I want you there,
	he's got some treasure there. If you don't find it
	you can live there till you do.

HECUBA comes through the dark entrance, drenched with blood.

AGAMEMNON	Barbarians.

MESTOR staggers in through the dark entrance, bleeding from his eye-sockets.

MESTOR	Gods are gone, it is I it is I alone!
	Only I was left and I *too*
	I was alone!
AGAMEMNON	You've changed somehow, what is it…
MESTOR	Witches coming out of the cave walls
	they slaughtered my two piglets like pigs!
	The queen – come here the queen – I'm going to skin you!
	Look on me, King Mestor, Mestor *of* Mestor!
	My name was my own island, we was we
	then I was I alone, I've no eyes,
	I had one eye so I could see the bodies
	of my boys, I heard the voice of my sweet bride
	Why is the blind eye crying
	when it can't see what was done? Then I was gone,
	I have no son! Avenge me!
AGAMEMNON	Hold him down.
MESTOR	Avenge me, there is no one to avenge me!
AGAMEMNON	Avenge you? I don't know you.
MESTOR	Agamemnon
	your enemies have done this!
AGAMEMNON	How could they,
	I *have* no enemies, the war is over.
	You murdered a young prince.
MESTOR	Your enemy!
AGAMEMNON	He was your guest.
MESTOR	He was a *Trojan* prince!
	You threw a little angel off a tower
	it had no wings.

AGAMEMNON   I didn't vote for that.
I don't vote, I'm a king.
Take this barbarian,
dump him on some rock so small he's always
beside himself.

CASSANDRA comes from the dark entrance, spattered with blood, and stands behind MESTOR. She wipes blood from his face, and presses balm to his eye-sockets.

MESTOR   Whose hands?
Whose hands on Mestor now?

CASSANDRA *[like a lullaby]* *She shall have a pebble necklace*
And the pebbles shall be rubies…

MESTOR   The bride can see what I can see,
she waited for me, waited for me…

CASSANDRA   Hush…
Hush I have to go now…

MESTOR   *Hush I have to go now…*

CASSANDRA   Away, away…

MESTOR   *Away now…*

CASSANDRA   Mother I have to go now…

MESTOR   *Mother…mother…*

MESTOR stamps a rhythm, breaks free, and though blind points straight at HECUBA.

MESTOR   *Mother is dancing on the deck*
Mother is screaming up a storm
Odysseus and his sailors stare
As mother howls the names of all
Her slaughtered puppies!

AGAMEMNON   Get him the fuck out.

MESTOR   *But now there's just a barking dog*
A-scrambling up the mast, oh!
The sailors can't believe their eyes
Now they believe a bitch can fly
Like a river down and down
To meet the sea and by and by

> *No ships will ever sail again*
> *Where this was seen, for fear of her*
> *Eternal screaming on the wind*
> *The queen of dogs, that dog's the Queen!*

KRATOS and TALTHYBIUS drag MESTOR out through the light exit.

AGAMEMNON   He said you could see that, Catfish, you could see
your mother's death. Can you?

CASSANDRA looks at HECUBA, who is staring into space, and she nods.

AGAMEMNON   Good, I'm glad. *[To HECUBA]* You're safe. She thinks my wife
will butcher me in my bath.
And of course I'd be concerned, but she goes on:
Athens will fall, of course, crumble to dust.
Italians rule the world, my personal favourite.
Men live a hundred years, fly to the moon,
grow flowers there. Little Catfish.
We're leaving now. Odysseus is coming.
He'll be here soon. Don't know what's keeping him.

*AGAMEMNON goes. CASSANDRA touches HECUBA. AGAMEMNON comes back
for CASSANDRA and leads her away through the light exit. HECUBA is left
alone in the gloom, spattered with blood, staring at nothing.*

HECUBA   Thou of Light…Thou of Light.
You are gone…you are gone.
There was nothing, there was nothing.
Show me something, Thou of Light…
Palidorus… Deiphobus…
Troilus…Thou of Beauty…
Creusa…Polyxena…
Thou of Battle…Pr – Pr – Priam…
Thou of Blood…He – He – He – Hector…
O Thou, Apollo thou,
O show me, show me, O…

HECUBA sinks to the ground, her body racked with sobs.

*Footsteps approaching, and faint light. HECUBA oblivious. It's TALTHYBIUS
who comes, through the light entrance, with a lamp. He is dressed for the*

long voyage home. He takes out a scrap of paper, reads it, folds it away. Finally he clears his throat and sings, from memory.

TALTHYBIUS   *I…er…stroll out in the morning sun.*
I'm…um…walking down Winemakers Street
I, er…gossip by the, the something gate…
And, murals of… the starry sky,
Old men drinking in the shade…
There's old men drinking in the shade!
Sisters fly…a kite they've made…
Blue is – the evening shade…
The temple steps are…
I…stroll out in the morning sun.

During this, HECUBA's sobs diminish and her body ceases to shake. She breathes again, brokenly, then steadily.

TALTHYBIUS places the lamp beside her, and withdraws through the light exit.

Slow fade to darkness.